AMONG
the
ENEMY

Great Lakes Books

A complete listing of the books in this series can be found online at
wsupress.wayne.edu

AMONG
the
ENEMY

A MICHIGAN SOLDIER'S
CIVIL WAR JOURNAL

EDITED BY MARK HOFFMAN

Wayne State University Press
Detroit

17 16 15 14 13   5 4 3 2 1

Library of Congress Cataloging-in-Publication Data

Kimball, William Horton, 1842–1920.
  Among the enemy : a Michigan soldier's Civil War journal / Edited by Mark Hoffman.
    p. cm. — (Great Lakes books)
    Includes bibliographical references and index.
    ISBN 978-0-8143-3471-3 (pbk. : alk. paper) — ISBN 978-0-8143-3853-7 (ebook)
    1. Kimball, William Horton, 1842–1920—Diaries.   2. United States—History—Civil War, 1861–1865—Personal narratives.   3. Michigan—History—Civil War, 1861–1865—Personal narratives.   4. United States. Army. Michigan Engineers and Mechanics Regiment, 1st (1861–1865)   5. United States—History—Civil War, 1861–1865—Engineering and construction.   I. Hoffman, Mark, 1963– editor of compilation.   II. Title.
    E514.9.K56 2013
    973.7'8—dc23

                                                                2012035460

Designed by Norman E. Tuttle
Typeset by Alpha Design & Composition
Composed in Adobe Caslon

To my Brothers in the Sons of Union Veterans
of the Civil War, Department of Michigan,
who keep alive the memory of those who served.
Yours in Fraternity, Charity, and Loyalty.

Contents

———◆———

Illustrations

————◆————

Maps

———◆———

Acknowledgments

I first read the Kimball manuscript while researching the Michigan Engineers and Mechanics in the 1980s. It has been a long journey from then to now, and many people have assisted along the way.

Nancy Obermayer was the first Engineers and Mechanics collaborator to concur with the importance of Kimball's recollections, and she prepared the very first transcription of the journal that I worked from for my book *My Brave Mechanics*. Nancy remains an inspiration in my continued research on the regiment.

Mark Patrick, former special collections director for the Detroit Public Libraries, was very encouraging from the start and eased the path for this journal to figuratively move from their collections to publication. His position has been ably filled by successor Mark Bowden, who helped push the project over the finish line. Thanks to both.

My daughter Alice Hoffman prepared a fresh transcription in preparation for this work and it confirmed both her solid skills and Nancy Obermayer's original work. Alice also prepared the index for this publication and I'm forever in her debt. My son Patrick Hoffman reviewed the chapter introductions and made many important suggestions. He is now a soldier in the U.S. Army, serving his nation in a very different kind of war than Kimball's, but also in the cause of freedom.

Max Miller was kind enough to allow me use of the only known photograph of William Horton Kimball in uniform. Bill Lowe first connected me with Max and has been a continued encouragement along the way. Both Max and Bill are dedicated members of the Sons of Union Veterans of the Civil War and keep alive the memory of Kimball and his comrades.

Several individuals went above and beyond the call of duty to provide illustrative materials. Photographer Elizabeth Tiffany greatly improved the postwar image of Kimball and produced the image of his gravestone. Photographer Tom Sherry did a great job with the images of Kimball's journal; it is easy to see why he came so highly recommended. Julie Meyerle of the Archives of Michigan was very helpful with several of the photographs from that collection and those reproduced from other sources. The excellent maps are the work of cartographer Sherman Hollander.

I also want to acknowledge the able and enthusiastic assistance of Carmen Tiffany of the Historic White Pine Village in Ludington. This fine institution, operated by the Mason County Historical Society, has a very rich collection. Special thanks to Dr. Bill Anderson, who first introduced me to this bountiful source of Mason County history and remains a constant encouragement.

The staff members of Wayne State University Press continue to be consummate professionals and tremendous partners to work with. I'd especially like to thank Kathryn Wildfong, editor in chief, for all of her help and support during this project.

Finally, many thanks to my wife, Ann, for putting up with the distractions of a lifelong study of the Civil War, and with me in general. I love you.

Introduction

In September 1861, eighteen-year-old laborer William Horton Kimball left his family's farm near Sandstone, Michigan, and enlisted in the Union army. Over the next thirty-eight months he served in one of the most important regiments Michigan offered to the Union cause—the First Michigan Engineers and Mechanics. Because it was not a combat unit, however, much of the daily life of the engineers has been overlooked by postwar historians. Fortunately, Kimball left behind a journal of his experiences that has been carefully preserved by the staff of the Burton Historical Collection at the Detroit Public Library.

The journal actually encompasses two different books, a memorandum volume and a bound ledger book. Both are in excellent condition, and the clear handwriting in ink has been well preserved. The first volume also includes a short biographical sketch prepared at the time by Kimball.

I first became aware of the Kimball journal more than twenty years ago while researching his regiment. The journal formed an important part of the story I told in *My Brave Mechanics: The First Michigan Engineers and Their Civil War* (Detroit: Wayne State University Press, 2007). I always felt, however, that the Kimball journal needed to stand alone to be fully appreciated.

During a lifetime of research, I have read scores of Civil War diaries and journals, both published and in their original form, yet I still consider Kimball's to be among the most interesting and valuable due to its rich content on the relations—both friendly and hostile—between Union soldiers and Southern civilians in occupied regions.

This is one of two bound volumes that Kimball used to record his service in the Michigan Engineers during the Civil War. The label was added when it was donated to the Burton Historical Collection. (Tom Sherry)

As military engineers, Kimball and his comrades were often assigned to work in the rear areas of the army. This isolation from the rest of the army left them open to hit-and-run raids by Confederate cavalry, semiregular partisans, and civilian guerillas. While Kimball's journal is a helpful account of the service of the Michigan Engineers, I believe its greatest importance lies in his description of the many encounters between soldiers in his company and the civilians in the countryside they were serving in. Though other units, such as infantry regiments, were also assigned duty in the rear, few spent as much of their war in areas where they were in direct contact—and often conflict—with enemy civilians. This makes the experience of the men in the Michigan Engineers particularly well suited to explore the occupier-occupied relationship.

In 1879, Kimball sat down to record his daily wartime activities. Several comments included in the journal clearly indicate this postwar composition, but the abundant detail makes it evident that he was working from some kind of daily account of his service written at the time. Furthermore, there is a large enough collection of wartime diaries and letters by men in Kimball's regiment and company to verify that

Kimball was basing his account on facts. On the rare occasion he gets his facts wrong, it is consistent with the limited perspective soldiers had of the war, usually reflecting a reliance on rumor or hope. Undoubtedly, Kimball may have chosen to omit some of the items that he recorded in his wartime notes, but the candor with which he assesses the abilities and service of his comrades and officers suggests that he held little back in the analysis and commentary found in the journal.

Kimball was very active in veterans' groups and a prominent elected public official in postwar Ludington, Michigan, yet there is nothing to indicate that he had any intention of preparing the journal for publication. Nor is there anything in his papers to suggest he ever shared the record of his service with anyone outside his family. In many ways, this journal could be compared with the letter books many veterans and their families gathered together after the war, composed in an effort to organize and retain a firsthand account of their experiences.

Although only a single part of the continuing flood of new Civil War material being published in the sesquicentennial of this seminal event, Kimball's journal helps fill one of the largest remaining holes in the modern Civil War narrative—the relationship between occupiers and occupied. From his story, we better understand the complex tensions that existed among the people who called themselves Americans, celebrated the same Independence Day and founding heroes, yet were mobilizing all of their resources to kill each other. Much has been written about what happened when this played out on a battlefield, but Kimball allows us to better understand the results when it happened away from the major military fronts.

I have intentionally tried to let Kimball tell his own story, providing only introductory and contextual material in each chapter and limiting footnotes. Kimball frequently makes passing mention of other soldiers in his company and regiment, but I have not further identified them through footnotes, unless this was necessary for clarity. Instead, first name or other identifying information is included in brackets at the first mention of a particular person or, more often, to differentiate individuals sharing the same surname. Kimball frequently mentions injured or wounded comrades, and I have not provided further information about their fate unless they failed to recover and remain with the regiment. Additionally, I have chosen not to intrude on the chapter introductions with frequent source footnotes, relying upon the bibliographic essay at the end of the book to provide information on sources used for this account.

Most of the family, including his parents, John and Elizabeth, retained the surname spelling of "Kimble." William Horton himself used both the "Kimble" and "Kimball" variants, generally settling on the latter later in life. For reasons of clarity, his later spelling is used for all members of the immediate family. Other family members, such as cousins also serving in the army, are referred to as in the original source.

Because this journal was the product of postwar transcription, it is much cleaner and easier to understand than is the case with unedited diary accounts. Misspellings and simple errors have generally been kept intact, although editorial brackets are used when necessary to provide greater clarity.

The story that follows is William Horton Kimball's. I have tried to present it to a larger audience and then remove myself from the scene to let him speak for his own service and that of his comrades.

1

Off to War

SEPTEMBER 22–DECEMBER 15, 1861

William Horton Kimball was born near Hector, Schuyler County, New York, on December 1, 1842. He was the sixth child of John and Elizabeth (Horton) Kimball. Both parents were native New Yorkers. The family also included William's siblings Anna (born 1827), Augustus (1830), Daniel (1834), Rachel (circa 1838), Amelia (1840), and Samantha (1848). Both Daniel and Rachel died young.

William was raised in the agricultural community around Hector, dividing his time between the original family farm and a second one his father bought in 1853 in nearby Burdett. Young Kimball attended local schools during the winter months. As he later recounted, this arrangement provided him with "a rather limited chance of obtaining an education which I always regretted but have the satisfaction of reflecting to know that my time was generally well improved while at school."[1]

Like so many others, John Kimball saw new opportunities to the west and decided in the fall of 1858 to move his family to Michigan. He purchased a farm in Jackson County for the then considerable sum of $2,200 and sold both farms in New York—the original one near Hector to his oldest son, Augustus. Anna and Augustus remained in New York with their young families, while John, Elizabeth, and their youngest children William, Amelia, and Samantha moved to Michigan.

---

1. "Biographical Sketch," William H. Kimball Papers, Burton Historical Collection, Detroit Public Library.

William made the trip separately, in charge of the family's household furniture, wagons, and livestock. Leaving on March 19, 1859, he journeyed by lake steamer from Dunkirk, New York, to Detroit, and then overland to Jackson County. Young Kimball made good time and arrived at the new farm on March 23, a week ahead of the others. This must have been a grand adventure for the sixteen-year-old. The rest of the family had a much easier journey, traveling by train to Niagara Falls and then on to Detroit by steamer and Jackson by rail. A local livery stable and hired driver took them the remaining few miles to their new home in a cold rain.

The Kimball family's new farm was located in section 3 of northern Spring Arbor Township, near the small post village of Sandstone and a few miles west of Jackson. The farm, including about 125 acres in cultivation, had been developed by horticulturalist Reuben Grant and already contained several structures. The Kimballs started immediately to improve upon what they had purchased, and when a census enumerator visited the farm in 1860, its value was estimated at $5,000.

One highlight of William's prewar life in Michigan was attending boarding school, housed in the buildings originally constructed for Michigan Central College in Spring Arbor. He was a student in the winter term of 1859–60. Near the close of the term, the structure housing the male students burned down and William and roommate Henry Fuller fled from the burning building, possessions in hand. This was the end of his formal education.[2]

After secession and the attack on Fort Sumter in April 1861, President Abraham Lincoln called on the loyal state governors for seventy-five thousand men to serve for ninety days to suppress the rebellion. Among the first to go from Michigan were the Jackson Grays, a prewar militia company under the command of Captain William Withington. This company was heavily engaged in the defeat at Bull Run on July 21, 1861, and Withington and several others were carried south to Richmond as prisoners of war.

---

2. Ibid. A Baptist college had been started at Spring Arbor, but it moved in 1853 to Hillsdale. The buildings remained largely vacant until the Free Methodist denomination established the forerunner of Spring Arbor University in 1873. It is not clear who was running the boarding school that William Kimball attended.

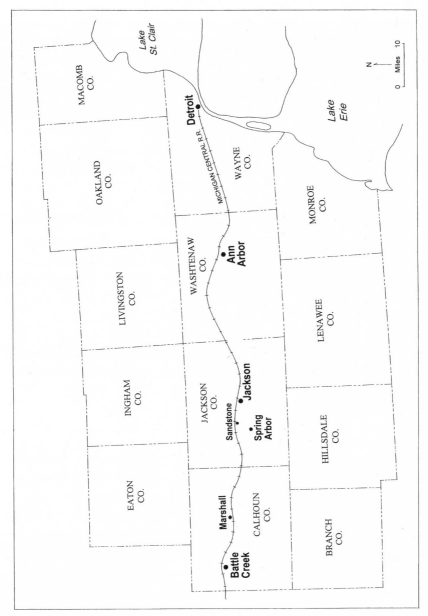

Kimball's Michigan, 1861. (Map by Sherman Hollander)

In the weeks and months that followed, military companies continued to form throughout the North, raised with the new and grim understanding that this war would not be won in a few short months with one decisive battle. Kimball's journal begins in September as he decides to enlist alongside friend and neighbor Schuyler McAlister.

Though McAlister soon changed his mind and withdrew from the roster, many of Kimball's prewar friends and neighbors did enlist together. This local pattern of recruitment characterized most Civil War companies organized in the early years of the war. Kimball's comrades Daniel and Charles Brown grew up on the farm just north of the Kimball place, and Thomas Spencer on the one to the south. Nearby were the Grants, Joneses, Hunts, and other farm families whose young men served alongside Kimball.

These men and others from neighboring farms and towns enlisted in a company formed by Enos Hopkins, a successful Jackson businessman and community leader. After great success in his native Connecticut, he entered the Jackson business community in the late 1850s as administrator of a large manufacturing concern. In particular, Hopkins became a friend and political ally of Jackson attorney Austin Blair, elected Michigan's governor in 1860.

Hopkins's unit was designated the Withington Rifles, in honor of Captain Withington, who remained in a Rebel prison in Richmond. Several of Hopkins's men had previously served under Withington in the Jackson Grays, and the two men were prewar business associates. Hopkins's men were assigned a place as Company H in the First Michigan Engineers and Mechanics regiment being organized by Colonel William P. Innes. Hopkins was almost immediately promoted to major in the new regiment. His place at the head of the Jackson company went to his senior lieutenant, Marcus Grant, a twenty-two-year-old veteran of the Jackson Grays.

Kimball and Grant had an interesting relationship. Their family farms were nearby and they certainly knew each other, despite Kimball's relatively short time in Michigan before the war. Kimball often accompanied Grant on social visits while the regiment was training in Michigan and was also a regular participant in Grant's various expeditions and escapades in the southern countryside after they reached the front. Yet Kimball's journal contains critical comments about Grant's abilities from almost the beginning of his service. Nevertheless, Marcus

Marcus Grant was Kimball's company commander and prewar neighbor. Kimball was frequently included in the expeditions and foraging parties that Captain Grant organized. (Archives of Michigan, Lansing)

Grant remained with the regiment the entire time it was in the service, earning high marks from his superiors and ending as the senior major in the regiment, despite criticism of some of his more spirited activities.

Solon E. Grant, Marcus's kinsman, was the original second lieutenant in Company H but was soon moved up to fill the vacancy caused by

Solon E. Grant, kinsman of Marcus Grant, was a longtime lieutenant in Kimball's company. (Sligh, *Michigan Engineers*)

the resignation of ill first lieutenant Edson Frary. Solon's vacancy was not filled for some time, so the two Grants were the sole officers physically present with the company during its first few months of service.

Each new regiment was assigned a point of rendezvous where it would be assembled and equipped and the men given rudimentary training in drill and military life. The Michigan Engineers rendezvoused at Camp Owen in Marshall, Michigan, under the command of Colonel William P. Innes and remained there until late December 1861. During that time, the Jackson company was officially designated Company H in the regiment.

Kimball's journal is full of references to the typical difficulties related to this process—officers with no or little military experience, chaos in the procurement of supplies and equipment, and the difficulty of quickly turning independent-minded civilians into soldiers so that they could be forwarded to the front in a rapidly expanding war. For example, one amusing incident is related in his journal entry for October 26, when two companies dumped tables loaded with unacceptable food onto the ground and refused to eat. Instead of being punished, the men accomplished their goal when the quality of rations was quickly improved.

The drill was hard work both for the men and the green officers. It made for comedic scenes despite the grim reality of its important purpose: to be able to move bodies of men around a battlefield. Significantly, however, there are no references in Kimball's journal, or that of other Michigan Engineers at Camp Owen, to target practice or any live fire drills. Neither was there any special training in the engineering skills they would shortly be expected to demonstrate at the front. That would have to come with time and rely heavily on prewar civilian experience.

In addition, Kimball's entries from Camp Owen introduce the great controversy over the men's pay—a problem faced by the five regiments of volunteer engineers taking to the field in the fall of 1861.[3] This dispute would drag on for more than a year, embroil the officers and men of the Michigan Engineers in charges and countercharges, and eventually lead to an outright mutiny. The pay problem greatly complicated the task

3. These regiments were the First New York, Fifteenth New York, Fiftieth New York, the Engineer Regiment of the West, and the Michigan Engineers and Mechanics. Regular Army engineer troops were already provided for in federal statute.

that Innes and his officers already faced and severely strained relations between officers and men.

With no formal arrangement for volunteer engineer regiments within the U.S. Army, recruiters offered wildly varying rates of pay—always in excess of that available to infantrymen. In most cases, they did so in good faith, believing the assurances they had received from federal officials, and their offers were in line with those being made by recruiters from other volunteer engineer units. The effect, however, was to create expectation for a rate of pay that would not and, under federal statute, could not be met. Hopkins, Innes, and the other officers in the regiment tried to clarify the situation. On October 3, Innes assembled the men and told them that federal officials had confirmed that skilled privates would receive $17 per month, $4 more than infantry privates. Though this was less than the men had been expecting, most of them made the decision to remain and accept it, not realizing that it was still more than what the army would actually offer in the coming months. Those who decided otherwise were allowed by Innes to leave. Once the men were sworn into federal service, however, they were in the army until death or discharge, and so after October 29 the officers and men were caught in a vice not of their making, but one bound to greatly complicate matters in a regiment of volunteers composed of prewar neighbors and friends.

Bit by bit, the necessary clothing, weapons, and equipment were obtained and issued to the men at Camp Owen. As November reached its end, it was clear that they would soon leave for the war. The men took advantage of final opportunities to obtain formal leave and visit family and friends, Kimball among them.

Sept. 22. Schuy McAlister was at our house and I obtained permission of father to enlist providing Mr. McAlister would let Schuy go, we being old associates were desirous of going together and sharing as much as possible the trials of such a life.

Sept. 23. Reuben Austin, a recruiting officer, was sent to enlist us. I went with him to McAlisters and Schuy and myself were sworn in at the same time and furloughed for one week. We then went to Mr. Hawkins to see Daniel Bennett, a brother of Mrs. Perry Hawkins, who was desirous to go with us but being young and quite small. Austin was doubtful whether he would pass muster or not but measured him and took his name. I always felt proud of having a hand in his enlistment for he proved himself an excellent soldier and returned Corporal Bennett.

Sept. 26. Attend the fair at Jackson and eat my first meal at Uncle Sams expense at the Exchange. Schuy had his name taken from the list, an opportunity being given those who wished to do so in consequence of a different arrangement being made in our pay. We enlisted with the understanding that all should receive $28.oo per month, the regiment to be called the Fusilier regiment.[4] The pay now offered was $19.oo per months and 40 cts extra each day to mechanics and laborer work or play, which would have made a better wages that the first had we got it.

Sept. 27. The young people met at our house in the evening and had a [dance?], each having some word of advice to give me and bid each farewell. I began to make arrangements to leave.

Sept. 30. My furlough having expired, father took me to Jackson where we were drilled by Solon E. Grant, who was acting as Orderly Sergeant. We took up our abode at the Exchange, where it was proposed we should eat at the [servants'] table, but as it was likely to create a row we eat with the white people. Some of the boys complained of hard fare already but there was no cause whatever for complaint as we had enough to eat and good food also. The boys of course were mostly strangers but all seemed to be a happy good natured set.

Oct. 1. We took the 10:30 train for Marshall, the rendezvous of the regiment. Mother and Amelia were at the cars to bid me good bye, not expecting to see me again unless I returned from the army which some said was doubtful as I was not old enough or strong enough to endure the hardships incident of a soldiers life. But small or medium sized men were as a general thing much the healthiest soldiers and could stand marching better. The other companies were formed each side of our path and thus in two ranks we marched in camp, which was the fairgrounds, proceeded by a few drums and fifes. We were marched to the dinner

---

4. The military term *fusilier*, or *fusileer*, was used during the American Civil War to refer to troops doing engineering or pioneer work. In the case of this regiment, it was dropped early in its service and the unit officially designated the First Michigan Engineers and Mechanics, usually shortened to First Michigan Engineers or Michigan Engineers and Mechanics. Kimball's understanding about pay was still very different than the army's intention, as he and his comrades would find out in the coming months.

table and one would not have wondered had there been some murmurings as the principal dish which was soup was a filthy looking and unpalatable mess of beef, bread and cabbage, mixed and cold, but the boys made the best of it. We were drilled in the afternoon and slept in an old circus tent at night or rather lay in it as there was so much noise song singing and story telling that sleep was impossible. Had straw to lie on and a few borrowed blankets for cover.

Oct. 2. We built us our bunks or barracks which were very dry and comfortable. A portion of the Co detailed in guarding. Each were armed with a club. Captain Enos Hopkins of our company was offered the position of Major of the regiment. He called the company out in line and said that with the consent of the men who had enlisted under him he would accept of the position but if it were their desire for him to retain his rank as Capt of the company he would do so. Of course, we were unanimous for his promotion. He thanked us and complimented us very highly for our improvement in drill and soldierly appearance. And we were proud of having as fine a looking and appearing man as him for our capt. He was a prominent member of the church, the Superintendent of a Sabbath School in Jackson, and a man of considerable wealth. But the army corrupted his morals to a considerable extent still he was the best field officer we had and a man who would sympathize with a private when he was in trouble and in fact his money was the bone and sinew of the regiment for the first six months.

Oct. 3. Captain Hopkins went east to be gone one week. A different arrangement was made in regard to the pay of the regiment. Mechanics now are to receive $19.00 per month and 40 cts extra each day they labored and laborers $15.00 per month and 20 cts for each day the labor. The officers proposed to conciliate the matter by putting down most of the men as mechanics asking each if they could drive a nail or bore an auger hole. Permission however was given for all who chose to have their names taken from the muster roll and leave to do so and quite a number improved the opportunity, the Kalamazoo Co nearly all leaving. But two or three left [from] our company.

Oct. 4. We were all examined by the Surgeon William H. DeCamp of Grand Rapids. But two were rejected in our Company they on account of size and age. It rained all night. We ate supper under shelter.

Oct. 5. We were measured in our stockings. My height was 5 1/2 ft. The tallest man was C C Vredenburg, he being 6 ft 3 1/2 inches. The shortest man was Dan Burr, he being 5 ft 3 1/4 inches. The required height was 5 ft 3 inches. A portion of our muskets and tents came. Drilled in the afternoon and while on a double quick several of us stumbled and fell and others falling over us creating considerable merriment.

Oct. 6. We had dress parade at 8 A.M. After supper we had some sport over a few oak burrs that lay around various companies trying to take them from each other. At night I attended a bible Class in one of the bunks. I heard a man speak and call another Slauson and watching him at the close of the meeting I spoke to him and found him to be Newell Slauson, an old York State school mate and a second cousin. We soon formed an acquaintance and were warm friends throughout our term of service.

Oct. 7. I was detailed as one of ten from our Co to stand guard. We were the first that had guns to use on guard and felt quite important. We relieved the old guard at 8 P.M. and were divided into three reliefs, being on duty two hours and off four. This system remained the same when we were in the service when it was possible to do so.

Oct. 8. We changed quarters from the barracks to tents. We were divided in five tents the largest men occupying No. 1, the next largest No. 2, etc. I came in No. 4. Drilled in the afternoon.

Oct. 9. We were drilled in the forenoon. At noon we were formed in line and escorted to dinner by the Marshall Cornet Band, after which we were dismissed to attend the county fair upon whose ground we were encamped. I met quite a number of acquaintances there.

Oct. 10. We were drilled in the forenoon and in the afternoon, the last day of the fair, we were presented with our colors. We stood in one formation for two hours and also marched in review.

Oct. 12. Newell Slauson and myself obtained furloughs to go to David Godfrey at Ceresco. We enjoyed sleeping in a feather bed very much although we had good straw to sleep on in camp which we would have considered a fine thing could we have had it at times when we were south.

Oct. 13. We returned to camp in the afternoon, visiting the city cemetary first.

Oct. 15. We drilled as usual. In the evening Captain Hopkins returned and our Company procured the Martial Band [Marshall Cornet Band] and escorted him to camp where he made some very appropriate remarks. A man belonging to Co. D died in the Hospital of Measles. We had a dance among ourselves on the camp ground.

Oct. 16. Drilled in the forenoon and in the afternoon I got excused to go downtown.

Oct. 17. Dan Brown & myself got a furlough to go home. I was weighed, my weight being 140 lbs, a gain of five pounds over my previous weight. We arrived in Sandstone about 5 P.M.

Oct. 18. I worked during the day and went to Parma at night to Perrins Panorama of the Holy Land and from thence to McAlisters.

Oct. 19. Worked very busy during the day.

Oct. 20. Went to church and took a ride in the evening.

Oct. 21. Returned to camp with Bill and Dan Brown.

Oct. 24. I was on guard. Was on the 1st relief which was always considered the best on account of sleeping.

Oct. 25. At 4 P.M. we were formed in line number about 900, headed by the band and with colors flying marched to the Depot to meet the 9th Infantry who were on their way South. The train stopped an hour. I saw some old acquaintances.

Oct. 26. We marched to breakfast as usual but found no sugar, miserable coffee, strong butter and poor meat. The boys got a little angry and Co B carried their table outdoors and emptied plates and victuals on the ground. Another company tipped their table over. Soon after the Commissary came on the ground (or rather the contractors for our board), and was groaned at and finally his team was stopped. Capt. [Wright] Coffinberry, officer of the day, ordered the crowd to disperse, which was of no avail. He then struck a man and came very near being mobbed for it. By dinner time the excitement had considerably abated and when we were marched to dinner everything was in style and all were well pleased. At supper we had tea which was a rarity.

Oct. 27. We formed a squad and marched down town to church. Had preaching in camp at 3 P.M. Went to church again in the evening. We drilled as usual.

Oct. 28. We drilled as usual. In the evening had a dance at Co D's quarters.

Oct. 29. The mustering officer (Capt Mizner, afterward Col of the 2nd Mich Cav) arrived and we were mustered in the United States Service.[5] No one was rejected in our company, but more or less from nearly all of the other companies. About thirty of the Marshall Company refused to muster, asserting that their Capt was incompetent to command.[6] At night the regiment was drawn up in line, the rear rank marching to the rear in open order, the front rank about facing and they pretended to drum them out of camp, but in reality escorted them out as the music preceded the men. Our company received about a dozen new recruits, making between 90 & 100 men in the company.

Oct. 30. It rained all day so we did not drill.

Nov. 1. We were vaccinated by the surgeon.

Nov. 2. It rained during the day. In the evening a number of us went to meet Captain Grant at the depot, he having been in search of a deserter from our company named [George] Waldo, who returned to camp the day before of his own accord. When Mark came he arrested him and put him in the guard house.

Nov. 3. Amanda Wall was in camp and we had a good sing. In the evening 38 from our company went to the Christian Church, all conducting themselves very gentlemanly. At the close of the services the minister shook hands with us all.

---

5. Captain Henry R. Mizner, Eighteenth U.S. Infantry, and later colonel of the Fourteenth Michigan, swore the regiment in. Kimball is confusing him with Captain John K. Mizner, Second U.S. Cavalry, later colonel of the Third Michigan Cavalry.

6. Captain Emery Crittenton overcame the stigma of this dispute, which arose from competing internal politics more than any question of his competence, and ended the war in 1865 as major.

Nov. 4. We were drilled by Capt. Grant. In the evening a subscription paper was circulated for the purpose of getting Capt. Grant a sword. Over one hundred dollars was raised for that purpose. The sword was purchased and presented, he receiving it without any thanks to the company for it and he soon hacked it up fencing with the other officers and finally a wagon ran over it, bending it badly. Maj. Hopkins furnished the money which was not paid to him for over a year as the boys refused to take their pay, and then not more that half who had subscribed were present, some having died, many left behind sick and others discharged, so those of us present proposed to foot the bill and settle the matter more for decency sake than for the admiration of the officer to who it was presented.

Nov. 5. Waldo had a sham trial by court martial and was fined $57.00, the amount expended in chasing him. He made a satisfactory explanation to the company, saying his wifes sickness was the cause of his leaving as he did. The company then volunteered to pay $50.00 of it each paying an equal share. But the whole thing being a sham affair we were never called upon to pay anything.

Nov. 6. I was supernumerary and had to guard the prisoners in the guard house.

Nov. 7. In the afternoon our company went to husk corn for a man by the name of Rowley. After husking he gave us a few apples and drink of water and we were marched back to camp. Some of the boys relieved him of some poultry just before going south. During our absence two brass cannon arrived for the artillery being raised by us.[7]

Nov. 8. Newell Slauson and myself got a furlough to go to Albion and remain four days. We went on the cars and stayed at Gallilands.

Nov. 9. We went in company with Sib and Randie Moore and Amanda Gardner to Jesse Gardners old farm. Had a splendid time.

Nov. 11. At night we took a freight train for Marshall. Reached camp about eight o'clock, having had an excellent visit. Dwight Hunt died of

---

7. Battery E, First Michigan Light Artillery, was originally raised to serve alongside the Engineers and Mechanics, but like many other similar arrangements between batteries and regiments, the connection was severed before seeing service.

Typhoid Fever. His mother was with him during his sickness and had his remains sent home. Four of the boys went as [pall] bearers.[8]

Nov. 12. Had regimental drill, which we found much more tiresome than company drill. Had a felon coming upon my thumb, but by having it lanced in time it soon healed.

Nov. 23. It snowed and froze all day. Chas and Dan Brown and myself went down town and had a good dish of oysters at Charley's expense, who was out visiting us. Charley had his picture taken and gave me which I carried for three years, little thinking that he would be my brother in law when I returned.

Nov. 24. Enough snow fell for sleighing. I was on guard but had a fire to stand by.

Nov. 28. It being thanksgiving day the regiment was formed in line and marched to the Methodist Church. We all had our new hats on each having a long [plume] or more properly (quill), a yellow cord with tassels, a brass eagle to loop up one side and a small brass castle completed the trimming for our hats. The castle was worn to distinguish us from the other branches of the service. After services we were marched back to camp where a sumptuous dinner, prepared by the ladies of Marshall and vicinity was waiting us, and of course we did ample justice to the good things set before us. Various mottoes were placed upon our plates and upon mine was a slip of paper upon which was written Revenge the death of noble Ellsworth.[9] How well I succeeded in doing so others must tell. One thing certain, I was not lacking in will to avenge his death. Our Capt took a whole turkey and passed it around, giving each man in his company a piece of it. In the evening Capt Grant and myself went home with Godfreys people and stayed all night. Had a good time.

Nov. 29. Capt. Grant and myself returned to camp on the 1:20 P.M. train. Gustavus Kimble came to see me and remained a few days. He

---

8. Dwight was the son of Ransom and Flavia Hunt, who buried him in Spring Arbor's village cemetery. Two other Hunt sons also died in the service. Dwight does not appear in regimental records because he died before being mustered into U.S. service and Kimball's journal is one of few references to his service and death.

9. Colonel E. Elmer Ellsworth of the Eleventh New York (Fire Zouaves) was killed by a Confederate sympathizer during the occupation of Alexandria in May 1861.

was a correspondent of the *Prairie Journal,* an agricultural paper published in Chicago. It gave him a bad impression of soldiering to see our style of living and when we left had but a little idea of ever becoming a soldier, but he afterwards enlisted in a N.Y. regiment and died while home on furlough before leaving the state.[10]

Dec. 7. It rained all day and night, taking off the snow and the frost out of the ground.

Dec. 8. As there was no water in camp about twenty of us a got a pass to go to the Kalamazoo River to wash and before leaving most of us went in the river, one or two plunging in first and daring the rest to follow. And each wishing to distinguish himself in some manner would follow suit. None of us however took a cold or suffered any only while in the water. In the evening a number of us went to church and returning we found man belonging to Co. A lying on the sidewalk drunk as we at first supposed and in fact he was so much so that he soon died.

Dec. 10. Capt & Lieut Grant, Newell Slauson, and myself and six others went to Ceresco to a dance. Amanda Wall inviting us there and Dr. Loewe's family would furnish the supper and the use of the hall being given to us by the owner, we hired livery teams and sailed out. Arriving there we took them somewhat by surprise. As the mud was so deep they did not expect us and there were no ladies present, but we took our teams and soon gathered in some ladies and went at dancing. Had a very pleasant time, an excellent supper, and arriving in camp about daylight, the muddiest looking objects I ever beheld.

Dec. 15. Charley Fowler and myself got a pass and went to an acquaintance of mine named Allen and got a good warm dinner, which a soldier knows well how to appreciate. We had to do some tall walking to reach camp before the time specified in our pass expired. Cos A and H received a special invitation to attend church at the Baptist Church in the evening. Both Co's were well represented.

10. Gustavus enlisted in the 161st New York on August 13, 1862, at Elmira, New York, and died of disease on November 20, 1862, at Odessa, New York. He and Kimball were first cousins.

2

Kentucky

By mid-December the Michigan Engineers were under orders for Kentucky, and they left Marshall amid great ceremony on the 17th. They marched as a body to the train station, loaded up onto a special train placed at their disposal, and said their good-byes. Kimball's account of that day reflected the mixed emotions of finally leaving for the front, knowing that many would not be coming home again. Two of his comrades didn't even survive the trip to Kentucky.

Their route by train was through southern Michigan and then on into Indiana to the Ohio River. At Louisville the regiment was divided into detachments of two or three companies each. The detachments were assigned to the scattered divisions of General Don Carlos Buell's Union Army of the Ohio. The Michigan Engineers were frequently divided into detachments and the terminology describing them can be confusing. In early 1862 they were often referred to as *divisions*, but this bore no relation to the usual use of that term to describe a force thousands of men strong. Likewise, the term *battalion* was frequently used to describe these temporary groupings of companies, even though the term did not officially apply to parts of the regiment until much later in the war.

Buell was organizing his command for an expected movement against Nashville, the capital of Confederate Tennessee and a major supply and manufacturing center. Confederate forces were arrayed against them on the likely avenues of advance through Kentucky and into Tennessee. Company H was to be part of a two-company

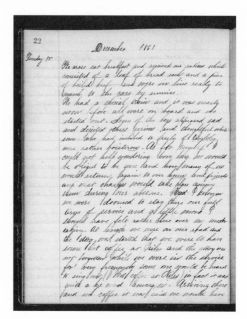

Kimball's journal entry for December 17, 1861, when he and the regiment left Marshall's Camp Owen en route to Kentucky. (Tom Sherry)

detachment, commanded by Major Hopkins, joined by Company C. They were ordered to report to Camp Wickliffe, riding by rail from Louisville to New Haven, and then marching the final ten miles over several days.

Hopkins and his men found themselves serving in Buell's Fourth Division, commanded by one of the sternest taskmasters in the Union army. General William "Bull" Nelson, a native Kentuckian, was a naval officer noted for his mercurial temper and large physical bulk. He had little patience for green troops and drove the men in his command hard, drilling them daily in the formations necessary for coordinated movement on the march and in battle. Despite the regular drill, the men still demonstrated their clumsiness with their weapons and Kimball notes several near escapes when their weapons discharged accidentally.

One of the most important jobs the men had in Kentucky at this time was the improvement of roads around nearby New Haven and New Buffalo. Designed for lower volumes of foot and vehicular traffic, these routes did not stand up to the hard wear of columns of Union troops. Kimball and the other Michigan Engineers especially enjoyed these work details because it got them away from the strict discipline of Nelson at Camp Wickliffe and the nonstop drilling.

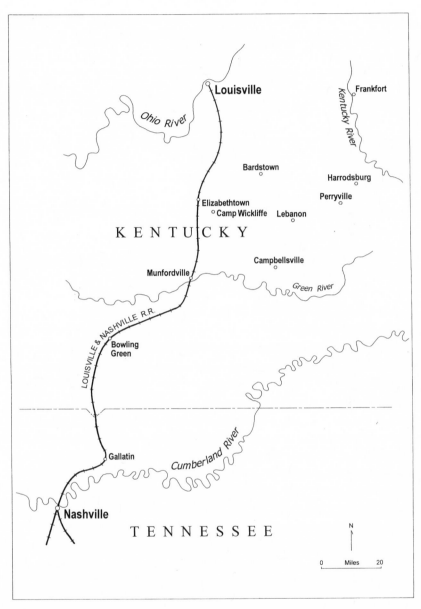

Louisville to Nashville. (Map by Sherman Hollander)

In addition to their first taste of military discipline and duties, these early weeks in Kentucky also exposed Kimball and his comrades to the complex relationship that existed between occupiers and occupied in wartime. This was especially true in divided Kentucky—a slave-holding state that remained loyal to the Union, but with its sons serving in both the Union and Confederate armies.

For most of the Michigan Engineers, this was the first time they had set foot in the South. In a war brought about by intense sectional rivalries, the Michigan men were quick to comment unfavorably on what they found, with Kimball no exception. His journal is replete with negative assessments, either from firsthand observations or stories told by others. The language, education, and manners of Kentucky residents all come in for criticism.

Kimball's journal is also filled with examples of how soldiers stole from local civilians, especially those considered to be sympathizers of the Confederate cause. He employs different words for the activity—"cramped" (January 23), "borrowed" (January 31), "captured" (February 11), for example—but they all had the same result. At the same time, Kimball and his comrades were frequently greeted warmly and fed well by local pro-Union civilians.

This reflected how soldiers actually operated within an official army policy that sought to bring wavering border-state residents into a stronger bond with the Union while surrounded by many whose sons were in the Confederate army. Attitudes and policy hardened as the war wore on, the casualties accumulated, and Union armies moved further into the Deep South. For now, however, there existed an uneasy truce between the army and civilians sympathetic to the enemy.

The ongoing dispute over pay was another topic of great interest to the men regularly recorded in Kimball's journal. Most of the men held firm against accepting the infantry pay, believing that it would jeopardize their claim to higher engineer pay, Kimball among them.

By the middle of February, the Confederates' defeats at Mill Springs and Forts Henry and Donelson rendered their defensive positions in Kentucky vulnerable, and they evacuated much of Tennessee, including Nashville. Buell's command, including Hopkins's two-company detachment at Camp Wickliffe, was ordered forward to a concentration at Nashville. After a long, winding journey, primarily by steamboat, Nelson's command reached Nashville on the 25th and settled down into camp as Buell's other forces arrived. Major Hopkins and Captain Grant hadn't moved fast enough for Nelson, and they were arrested en route, an incident which Kimball faithfully records in detail.

Dec. 16. Orders were received for us to march and preparations were accordingly made. Extra guards were detailed to keep the men in camp. About half the men managed to get out, myself among the rest. I crawled under the fence the guards not being desirous of keeping anyone in against their will. I returned about midnight and found some of my Ceresco friends awaiting to bid my good bye.

Dec. 17. We arose ate breakfast and received our rations, which consisted of a loaf of bread each and a piece of boiled beef and we were in line ready to march by sunrise. We had a special train and it was nearly noon before all were on board and we started out. Some of the boys appeared sad and dejected, others serious and thoughtful, while some who had imbibed too freely of tangleleg[1] were rather boisterous. As for myself, I could not help wondering how long we would be obliged to be gone and how many of us would return again to our homes and friends and what changes would take place among them during our absence. Had I known we were doomed to stay there our full term of service and a little more, I would have felt rather blue over my undertaking. At length we were on our road and the story was started that we were to have some hot coffee at Niles and the story was not forgotten while we were in the service, for very frequently some one would be heard to sing out (Hot coffee at Niles) in fact it was quit a bye word among us. Arriving there and no coffee, it was said we would have a good warm meal at Mich City at which place we arrived at sundown (but no supper was awaiting us and some of the boys replenished their canteens with Ready go down,[2] which they said answered every purpose. At Mich City we took the New Albany & Salem R.R. for Lafayette, at which place we were to have some hot coffee. We arrived there about 10 P.M., where a portion of the 40th Ind and a large number of citizens were awaiting our arrival but what was better, an abundance of coffee was in readiness for us which revived us up considerable. I filled my canteen

1. A nineteenth-century slang term for liquor.
2. Presumably another term for liquor.

with it. The night was splendid as was the day. The moon was dull and it being very clear we could see the country almost as well as in the day time. The appearance of a woman in a door or window with a hand-kerchief or dishcloth in her hand was all that was required to produce tremendous cheering and an officer passing through one of our cars would be almost as deafened with the cheering and one year after that many of them could not have raised such a shouting among the men short of performing at the end of a tight rope and the boys wouldnt shout at a regiment of women waving flags. Charley Brown accompanied us as far as Paw Paw & little thought he would be a brother in law when I returned.

Dec. 18. We arrived in Indianapolis at 5 A.M. and were detained there until daylight, but a guard was stationed at the doors to keep all inside, but some jumped out the window. We were here divided in two trains and proceeded to Jeffersonville, arriving about noon and after receiving one days ration of bread we went on board the ferry boat and crossed the Louisville. While crossing Col. Innes was called for a speech and in his remarks he said he would follow us through our campaign and upon the field of battle. Maj. Hopkins was next called for and he said that he proposed to lead us instead us following and as we were about to set foot on a hostile shore we would expect to meet with opposition and he hoped that Col would not be found wanting in courage to lead us through all opposition. It all passed off as a joke the Maj. being considered the best stump speaker, but neither were found wanted courage sufficient to lead us in time of battle. On reaching the Ky shore we disembarked and were formed in line and marched through the city receiving many cheers and the next morning a complimentary notice from the Louisville Journal to the effect that we were the finest body of troops that had yet passed through the city. We pitched our tents and cooked our supper as best as we knew and make awkward work of it. The day was very warm and the night cold and I think I was never more utterly exhausted than that night as I had had no sleep for two nights. I was very restless in my sleep, getting up once and crowding in bed with another fellow, but soon got froze out there and waking up retreated to my own nest again. I took a very severe cold and altogether I considered soldiering a rather serious job, but was not discouraged by any means and consoled myself with the vain idea that the war would not last long.

Jacob Shaffer was complaining some before we left Mich and died during the night of congestion of the brain. He seemed to be an estimable man and his death was much regretted in the company. He left a wife and several children. A man also belonging to our company named Deteroe [Joel Detterow], who started ahead with the teams and wagons, fell off the train when within two miles of Jeffersonville and was run over by the train, from the effects of which he soon died. It seemed to cast a gloom over the company, losing two men so soon.

Dec. 22. I was quite unwell having a chill and fever. It stormed all day and was very muddy.

Dec. 23. We learned the reg't was to be divided and sent to the different commanders for work. The 1st Div commanded by Col Innes consisted of Cos B E & I and were sent to Munfordville under Gen McCook. The 2nd Div under Lt Col Hunton consisted of Cos D F & G and were sent to Gen Thomas in Eastern Ky. The 3rd Div was commanded by Maj Hopkins Cos C & H composing it and the 4th under Capt. Yates were Cos A & K and were sent to Bacon Creek under Gen Mitchell. The 2nd left the 25th.

Dec. 26. Our Division struck tents at 5 A.M. and reached the L&N Depot at 7 A.M. We got on the train and arrived in New Haven about noon, nothing of interest transpiring on the route except knocking a cow off the track in a ditch. We were very much afraid to buy anything of the natives for fear of getting poisoned generally inducing them to eat some first, but we got bravely over that before our time was out. We marched a short distance from the town and Maj Hopkins said according to a general order we must load and march in platoons to guard against surprise, which seemed rather absurd to us after more experience. We went about two miles and stopped to camp but before we got our tents up there came up a heavy shower, which soaked us and wet our guns which were Harper's Ferry Muskets. Our camp was on the bank of Knob Creek in a very pleasant place and the Maj concluded to remain a few days. It was but 1/4 of a mile to the spot where the school house stood in which President Lincoln went to school, but two miles from where his father resided. The water of the creek was very clear and cool, it being a mountain stream in every sense of the word. The scenery was very varied and beautiful. It froze hard at night but we had straw to lie on.

Dec. 27. We had some target shooting and then cleaned up our guns. Had no guards during the day but several at night.

Dec. 28. I cooked in John Clarks place, he being unwell. The boys had some more target shooting in the forenoon and in the afternoon an old fellow said he would furnish a turkey for the boys to shoot at to be set up 40 rods off and the one that hit it should have it. The first shot was fired by Co. C and the turkey was hit the first shot fired. He then set up another 80 rods off and about half of each company had fired at it when [Ezra D.] Hathaway of our company hit it. He would not get up another for the rest of us to have our skill at. He was surprised at the accuracy of the shots with such guns.

Dec. 29. George Green, Mic Chamberlain and myself took a walk upon one of the knobs and were considerably interested, especially Green, who had always lived in Mich and such hills and rocks he had never seen before. He saw a chestnut burr and picked it up but dropped it much sooner that he raised it. Some loose rocks came tumbling down the mountain and that scared him considerably. We stopped at two houses and to show us proper respect they brought on some corn whiskey, drinking first themselves to let us know it was not poison. It was customary for them to set whiskey before their guests.

Dec. 30. We picked up and marched eight miles to Nelson's division which was camped on the pike beyond Muldraughs Hills and twelve miles from Green River. I got my knapsack on the wagon as I did not feel well.

Dec. 31. Gen Nelson came up and ordered us to move our camp about twelve rods and pitch the tents as regulations directed, which we did. One of the boys saluted him but not doing it quite to the taste of the old general he paid no attention to it. He found two of the boys down the pike and inquired what command they belonged to which they told him. He ordered them back and told the Maj the next he caught he would arrest and punish.

Jan. 1. The division was attached to the 41st Ohio to draw rations and drill. Col [William B.] Hazen (after Maj. Gen.) was in command of the brigade. The Co's drilled in the forenoon. I was on guard and as I was about to be relieved at 10 P.M. Elic [Alexander] Matheson who was on a neighboring post in full view of where I stood, challenged a dog that had passed me but a few minutes previous and he not halting as commanded fired at it supposing it to be a man trying to shoot him. Soon the long roll began to beat and the whole division was out under arms ready for fight. Matheson was much excited and remarked after he got to the tent if he had only thought to take aim he might have hit it. He soon after got his discharge and received much sympathy at home by showing a scar which he said was occasioned by a wound received while hunting guerillas but was simply the scar of a large boil he had while in the tent with me. He was very well educated but otherwise not amounting to much. We afterwards learned it was the intention of Nelson to create an alarm and get the boys out to see how well they would appear and Matheson's firing only hastened it a little.

Jan. 2. A fellow in Co. C snapped a cap on an empty gun as he supposed but being loaded it went off slightly wounding one of the boys in a neighboring tent, tearing the cap from his head.

Jan. 6. We went on battalion drill with the 10th Ohio. Our brigade consisted of the 41st O.V. [Ohio Volunteers], the 46 & 47 Ind. and 6th Ky. I sold my watch to John Clark, agreeing to wait for my pay until pay day.

Jan. 7. We were sent to cut a road through the woods a mile in length for us to go out on battalion. Mic and myself strayed off and found some walnuts under a tree and had a good feast.

Jan. 13. Was the coldest day we had yet seen in Dixie. Had a company drill in the forenoon and battalion in the afternoon. Snowed at night.

Jan. 14. Snow was about an inch deep but we drilled as usual. It rained during the night; the tent leaked some but not to annoy us much.

Jan. 15. I was on guard. It rained all day and half of the guards were withdrawn so we stood but four hours.

Jan. 16. We were on battalion drill with the 41st Ohio in the mud ankle deep. It was a shame to drill in such weather but of course we had nothing to say. Some excitement in among us about our pay, some declaring they would go home if not paid.

Jan. 19. I was quite unwell in the forenoon but attended preaching in the 41st in the afternoon. About sunset one of the boys belonging to the 41st was buried with military honors. The order of the procession on such occasions was 1st the band with drums muffled, next the corpse or coffin covered with the American flag, then the escort with arms reversed, then the officers and men, the band playing some funeral march in very slow time. After lowering the coffin in the grave the guard fires three volleys over the grave, then a prayer and some remarks by the Chaplain if any is present, and the procession returns to camp in quick time.

Jan. 20. I was one of 12 or 15 detailed from the two co's to go to New Buffalo and repair a sluice and the pike. Did a good days work. During our absence the paymaster arrived offering us $13.00 per month. The men were drawn up in line and voted whether they should take it or not, all being in favor of $17.00 or nothing. He paid us the latter. Brown, a clerk of the sutler, arrived with some goods.[3]

Jan. 21. The same who were sent before were again sent to work on the road. The news of Zollicoffer's defeat and death reached camp.[4] We heard the cheering three miles from camp. Brown trusted the boys and some went in heavy [with debt].

Jan. 23. All that were able went at work repairing the pike, which was a macadamized[5] one but had washed in some places. I was not very well and remained in camp and cooked. I made a pot pie of some geese the boys cramped the night before. It was very nice and light and we relished it well, being quite a change from bacon and hardtack, as the crackers were called by the soldiers.

3. The regimental sutler was a merchant who received special permission to travel with the regiment and sell goods to the soldiers. He filled an important niche, selling such things as newspapers, stationery, stamps, and tobacco, along with food delicacies. Sutlers often also sold liquor in violation of the regulations.

4. Confederate general Felix Zollicoffer was killed, and his command routed, by forces under General Thomas near Fishing Creek along the Cumberland River in eastern Kentucky. Lieutenant Colonel Hunton and Companies D, F, and G were part of Thomas's force but were not engaged in the fighting. The fighting was also referred to as the battle of Mill Springs.

5. At the time of the Civil War, macadam was a form of road construction with three layers of crushed stones laid on a crowned subgrade and with side drainage ditches. Each layer was compacted, causing the stones to lock together and provide a higher-quality roadbed.

Jan. 24. Two of the teams with several of Co. C's men went to New Haven to work there. The rest of us worked near camp. At night I went a half a mile from camp to get some milk and soon the table was set and I invited to partake, which of course I could not refuse although it made me late to camp. When returning I heard a noise in the brush and the thought of guerillas struck me as I was unarmed, but I soon found it to be hogs. I hastened on to camp pretty lively though. Had tea, biscuit, butter, honey, pickles, etc, for supper.

Jan. 26. We had a number of visitors during the day. One old gentleman invited Clark, Fowler, and myself to his house to eat Sourkrout. We went just at night and had a good feast, also a pleasant visit. Each of us had a revolver with us.

Jan. 28. We worked on the road. I stayed to watch the tools at noon while the rest went to their dinner, and going to a neighbors I got a good warm meal. Traded some coffee for Sorghum.

Jan. 30. I was on guard at the quartermaster's and froze to some coffee and rice.[6]

Jan. 31. Co. H had orders to be ready to march at 9 A.M., leaving one tent with the sick in it behind. We were to repair the road as we went along. We went about seven miles and camped. Our tents were Sibleys and were so crowded (twenty-four to a tent) that when one turned over all had to do the same as they lay spoon fashion. Mic and myself slept in [*illegible*] wagon, which though rather cold was more agreeable than to be so crowded. Bill Haynes and some others went and borrowed some poultry of the man on whose farm we were camped, for which the Maj had to pay to avoid getting in trouble, but he found no fault in so doing.

Feb. 1. We started early to repair the roads leaving our tents behind. When within a mile of the river we heard several shots fired and the cavalry came in saying our pickets had been fired on.

Feb. 2. We returned to camp sorghum, as it used to be known by us. Mic, Charlie Fowler and myself squaded off by ourselves and got some milk for our pains. The name of the division camp was Camp Wickliffe.

6. Apparently a humorous reference to taking some of the food stores he was supposed to be guarding.

Feb. 3. It being rainy the home question was argued pretty strongly, some thinking we would soon go home on account of their not offering us but $13.00 per month.

Feb. 4. We had a general inspection and were drilled by the Maj.

Feb. 5. We marched back to Camp Wickliffe much against our will as our privileges there were but few.

Feb. 6. A letter was rec'd from Co. A saying they had also been offered $13.00 per month but refused it. It set our camp in commotion again.

Feb. 7. The 15th brigade belonging to Nelson's division moved toward Green River. I was one of twenty sent to work on the pike again. We called Maj. H our pathmaster.

Feb. 8. The 19th brigade, to which we belonged, had orders to move the following day but the order was countermanded. Maj. Hopkins was in Louisville. Twenty of us from Co. H and an equal number belonging to Co. K, 6th Ohio or Guthrie Greys [and] Nelson's favorites, were sent nearer New Haven to work on the pike. Several teams accompanied us and we took the tent, which we put up and rested the rest of the day.

Feb. 9. The day being beautiful the officers concluded we must work, which we did not relish very well, but did a good days work having some corn oil to work. The night was very cold.

Feb. 10. The Maj returned from Louisville and did not like the idea of the Ohio boys working with us.

Feb. 11. It was stormy in the forenoon so we did not work. Some of the boys captured eleven stray chickens, making us a good dinner. Potatoes and Corn Oil was also abundant. We were reinforced by about 30 more of Co. H.

Feb. 13. An order came for the Ohio boys to return to camp. Also one from Capt Grant to the Maj for us to return, but the Capt by mistake put in a scrap of blank paper instead of the order. The Maj and Capt Coffinberry thinking there was some mistake returned to camp.

Feb. 14. At 1 o'clock A.M. an order came from camp for men to return immediately. There was two inches of snow on the ground and very muddy underneath it. We reached camp at 7 A.M. just as our brigade was leaving. Charley Fowler and myself strayed off from the rest and found two cows which we milked and had a good breakfast. We were to march at 12 M. [noon] but got only three miles on account of the wind. The night was *the coldest* of the season. Wagons that were left standing in the mud and even mules had to be chopped out the next morning but ours were left on hard ground. We had good warm beds as there was a stack of oats near where we camped and we appropriated them for our beds. The owner complained of his loss and the Maj paid him for them out of his own pocket. I think I never felt more refreshed after a nights rest than I did after that one. We found an old bake kettle which was very serviceable to us afterward cooking our grub.

Feb. 15. We were called out at 4 A.M. and marched at 6 A.M. The ground was frozen hard and we had no difficulty to get along with the wagons. We passed through Hodginsville and Elizabethtown which were very pretty villages and overtaking the 19th Brigade we proceeded with them until we camped. The boys some of them were completely tired out. In our tent there were about twenty and of that number only five of us could be mustered to pitch the tent, two of whom were teamsters. There was snow on the ground and we could get no straw to lie on but spreading down our blankets and keeping up a good fire in the stove we rested very well.

Feb. 16. We got started again at 6 A.M. and carried my knapsack most of the way but finally got it on a wagon. Half of the Company were in the rear scattered along many of them on the wagons riding. We reached West Point about sunset the snow still remaining on the ground. West Point abounded in mud in quantities to suit the most fastidious.

Feb. 17. It was quite cold and foggy. In the forenoon we built a road to the boats. At 3 P.M. we had orders to strike tents and pack up preparatory to going on board a boat. The Maj went down to see what boat we were to take. The Capt of the boat said it could not carry us on account of having a load already. The Maj reported the same to Gen Nelson who told him he could load on that boat or remain behind and be reported to Gen Buell. The Maj counseled with the rest of our officers and finally concluded to remain and risk the consequences. Accordingly we repitched our tents and got settled again when Nelson and staff rode up he in a great passion said he had arrested the Maj and Capt Grant and ordered the tents struck immediately but not moving quite quick enough to suit him he began cursing and said if we were not at the boat in half an hour we would send a regiment up and march us down at the point of a bayonet. The old fellow was fairly purple with rage and had one peculiarity about his swearing. He would always (damn his own soul). We reached the boat at dusk nearly covered with mud and set about loading our troop on board. The officers said it would take until 1 A.M. for us to get loaded but all got on board before 10' oclock and shoved off with the other boats at 10 P.M. There was twenty boats in the fleet and ours the *Lancaster* was one of the fastest among them. We felt rather blue as we were aware we had incurred the displeasure of Gen Nelson and the Capt and Maj were left behind under arrest. Capt Coffinberry of Co C was in command.

Feb. 18. We stopped at Cannelton for coal, also at Evansville. Weather clear and cool. Some racing among the boats.

Feb. 19. We reached Smithland at the mouth of the Cumberland and the orders were countermanded and we started up the Ohio again. Considerable racing, especially between our boat and the *Star of the West* who were evenly matched. We passed several boats loaded with troops and stores. Weather cold and stormy.

Feb. 20. We awoke in Evansville. Left at 7 A.M. up the river. Stopped at Newburg to repair our engine. The *Diana,* with Nelson on board, came along and he gave orders to return to Evansville and from there to Paducah. Our cooked rations gave out we had no means of cooking any so we eat our pork raw.

Feb. 21. We reached Paducah at 11 A.M. There was (26) boats there including ours loaded with troops and munitions of war. The river rose during the night three feet. I parted with my last three cents for a pie. We learned of the capture of Fort Donelson and after learned that we were started to participate in the fight but were too late. Our returning up the river was through fear the enemy might overpower our forces at Bowling Green and march on Louisville.

Feb. 23. We started up the Cumberland River at 8 A.M. Corporals [David] Shumway and [David] Johnson were chosen to act as Serg'ts and [Charles] Marion & [Albert] Vanderwarker as Corporals. I was detailed as cook for the ensuing week. Could cook nothing but got a kettle of coffee made occasionally by the boat's cook. Eat our meat raw.

Feb. 24. We reached Fort Donelson during the night and left at 7 A.M. Passed the ruins of the large rolling mill that had just been destroyed. They were built by the rebs to manufacture shot and shell. Passed [General U. S.] Grant on the *Tigress*. Passed breastworks the rebs had erected at Clarksville and one or two other places saw guns mounted and some had been rolled down the bank in the river.

Feb. 25. The day was beautiful and the river the highest it had been known since 1847. We reached Nashville at 9 A.M. and our division was the first to take possession of the city. A gunboat led the van up the river. Our boat was one of the first in the line. Some appeared pleased to see us and one man I noticed held up a flag in one hand and raised the other as if taking an oath to sustain it. An old Irish woman jumped up and down shouting as we came in. It was a day we felt proud of. Some of Buells men were on the opposite side of the river but none in Nashville. Gen Nelson took the 6th Ohio and raised the colors on the State House which was a splendid edifice.

Feb. 26. I got a pass for Dan Brown and myself to go uptown and trade some coffee for bread. Had some Tenn shinplasters[7] given me with which I could purchase anything to the values of the amount I had. We unloaded during the day and went about two miles to encamp.

Feb. 27. We moved our camps about a mile and stuck up our stakes near our old friends headquarters, Gen Nelson. I did my washing. Our entire trip was (610) miles.

---

7. Shinplasters were paper money issued by a variety of public and private institutions in low denominations. They helped to fill the void caused by the hoarding of coins, which were worth more than face value because of the demand for metals in war production.

3

Nashville to Corinth

MARCH 1–MAY 30, 1862

Nashville was a city of some seventeen thousand in 1860, larger than any in Michigan save Detroit, and the Michigan Engineers took full opportunity to play tourist. Kimball and most others visited the new state capitol building and the grave of President James K. Polk. The widowed First Lady was a tourist attraction in her own right and is frequently mentioned in Union soldiers' letters and diaries from this time.

There were several bridges to be repaired and other projects to be completed in the Nashville area. Perhaps the most interesting project was a river expedition to capture Southern railroad rolling stock. Since Southern railroads used narrower gauge tracks than those in the Northern states, Union supply officers were desperately scrounging for any captured rolling stock that could be put to military use on captured rail lines. An engine and several cars had been left stranded several miles from the Tennessee River, on a short stretch of the incomplete Nashville and Northwestern Railroad. Innes was sent with one hundred of his men to bring them to Nashville by boat for use on the railroad there. Kimball didn't accompany the expedition, but he noted the connection between efforts to unload the captured rolling stock upon their return and the continued lack of pay.

The pay issue continued to anger the men. There were more rejected offers of infantry pay and threats not to work unless given engineer pay. Innes and his officers took more severe action against the ringleaders, reducing some in rank and confining others in the guardhouse. On

April 2, the majority refused when ordered to march. Post commander and Brigadier General Ebenezer Dumont threatened to have the mutiny leaders shot, but he did promise a hearing of their grievances. With a night to think it over, some of the men's anger cooled, and most of them left Nashville on the 3rd, Kimball among them. Reaching Columbia, they joined with other men from the regiment already at work repairing bridges over the Duck River.

The movement from Nashville was part of a general advance by Buell's army toward an intended union with General U. S. Grant's forces at Pittsburg Landing on the Tennessee River. The Michigan Engineers moved in the rear of Buell's column, helping the army wagons over rough spots. They were not present when the lead divisions of the Army of the Ohio were thrown into the combat around Pittsburg Landing and Shiloh Church, as Grant's forces were recovering from a surprise Confederate attack on April 6.

Eight companies of the Michigan Engineers with Buell's command finally arrived at the banks of the Tennessee River on April 11 and were across and set up in camp by the 15th. From there, they were detailed to build steamboat landings and construct bridges across swollen creeks surrounding the growing Union encampment. By this time, a Union force of almost one hundred thousand men under Major General Henry Halleck was gathered near the old Shiloh battleground, preparing to move to the southwest against the Confederate base at Corinth.

A cautious man by nature, Halleck was determined not to be surprised as Grant had been, and so he moved slowly, covering only twenty miles in as many days. The rugged terrain, limited road network, and rain also combined to slow the columns and keep the Michigan Engineer working parties very busy. Kimball and his comrades labored daily in the rain and mud. By late May, Halleck's forces were on the outskirts of Corinth, but the Confederates slipped away with little loss, preferring to wait for more equal odds and a battlefield of their choosing.

The Michigan Engineers were exposed to hostile fire only briefly, without loss, but they continued to suffer from disease and the rigors of military service. By the end of May, almost half of the original one thousand members of the regiment were dead, discharged, or sick in Union hospitals. Kimball records the death and burial of one of them, his friend Perry Benson, shortly after their arrival in Nashville.

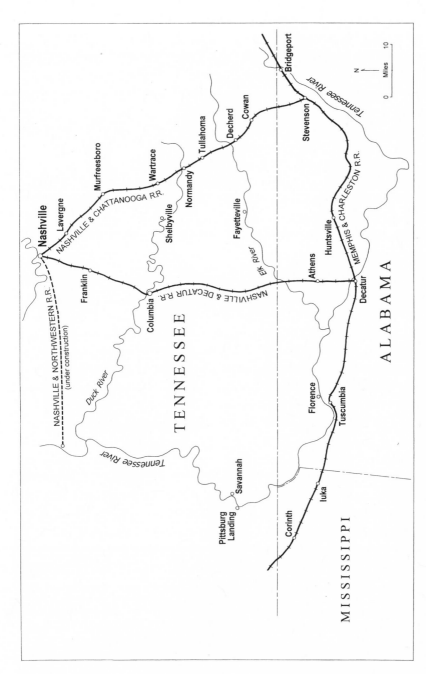

Nashville to the Tennessee River. (Map by Sherman Hollander)

Mar. 1. The day warm and beautiful.

Mar. 2. Some of Co. C's men strayed out in the country and found a lot of corn and tents left by the rebs. Had a heavy shower which overflowed many of our tents but ours being well ditched was dry. Some of the boys when they awoke were half covered in water.

Mar. 3. It was very cold, snowing some. I was on guard and was obligated to have a fire. Perry Benson died of Typhoid Fever at 4 P.M. He was taken while on the boat and was a splendid good fellow.

Mar. 4. I was one of the bearers at Perry's funeral. The rest of our regiment with Capt Grant and Maj Hopkins arrived. They had no charges preferred against them and were released when Nelson got over his passion. The other detachments camped with the commands they were attached to.

Mar. 5. Michael Connell of the 24th Ohio had been sentenced to be shot between 4 & 5 P.M. on today, he having been tried by court martial for shooting a corporal while on guard. In the afternoon we were marched to the camp of the 41st Ohio and forming on their left we were marched to the ground chosen for the execution. There were (8) regts of Infty (3) companies of Artillery and some cavalry present. In about an hour after our arrival the prisoner was brought in the procession being formed thus: 1st Brass Band playing a dirge, then a guard of eight men. Next the coffin and bearers, followed by the prisoner who marched between two clergymen and another guard of Eight and Corp [corporal] bringing up the rear. After marching him thus in front of all the reg'ts present they halted on a piece of ground affording all a good view and read his sentence. He then knelt in prayer and the Clergy beside his coffin. A handkerchief was then tied over his eyes but was soon removed and we all supposed he had been pardoned, but after he had said a few words it was replaced, the signal given and Michael Connell was no more.

When shot he sunk back upon his coffin and set upright a second or two and then rolled off on his side. He was examined by two surgeons who pronounced him dead, four balls having passed entirely through his breast. We were all marched near the corpse as we left. He was shot more for an example than for the crime he committed, as he did not hit the corp when he shot at him.

Mar. 6. I was on guard. The weather very cold. Pay rolls were brought around and we requested to sign them, but all refused. Col Innes came and told us, among other lies, that Gen Buell had issued an order to the effect that if we did not sign the payrolls and get our pay, we would forfeit all of it. He was groaned and hissed at considerably.

Mar. 7. Some of the sick signed the payrolls and a few others, in all 15 or 20. They offered us but $13.00 per month.

Mar. 8. I had a bad cough and reported sick. A report was circulated that all who chose could enlist in the regular army, receiving $25.00 bounty down and a furlough of 30 days. Lieut [Arthur] Conley of Co. K was transferred to Co. H as 2nd Lt and Lt Grant promoted 1st Lt in place of [Edson] Frary, who resigned on account of health. Conley had the consumption and was never with us.[1]

Mar. 9. An order came for all who chose to go to the Depot and go at work. But few went.

Mar. 10. I was quite unwell. We drew one days ration of soft bread which was quite a luxury for us.

Mar. 14. Chas Fowler and myself got a pass and went to town. We visited the cemetery and saw the graves of several noted men. Among others Gen Zollicoffer and several ex Governors of the State. The cemetery was beautifully laid out and adorned with trees and shrubbery. Also visited the grave of James K. Polk, who was buried in his door yard. His wife was president of a society of ladies whose object was to induce men to join the rebel army and those who did not were the recipients of a hoop skirt or some token of their disapproval. She also alarmed her negro woman so in regard to the Yankees coming that she killed her child and then cut her own throat. Saw Gen. O. M. Mitchell the astronomer. Went to the depot and as it rained we staid over night with the regiment.

Mar. 15. The rain carried off the bridge our boys had been building. We eat dinner with Rosenfield,[2] an acquaintance of mine, and did justice to

1. Neither man lived long after leaving the army. Frary died in Jackson in May and Connelly in Grand Rapids in October. Kimball misspells the latter's surname.
2. Probably John Rosenfield, Company H, Third Michigan Cavalry, Jackson County. He died in the service in September 1864.

the victuals set before us. When we returned to camp we found we had been marked absent without leave, but having a pass from Capt Grant stating we were detained at the depot made it alright.

Mar. 16. My eyes were swollen nearly shut, so I was excused from standing guard. Got some tea from Hospital.

Mar. 17. We were ordered to the city to camp. Green and I were left to guard some hay. Milked some cows. The Col took about 100 men and went down the river after an engine and some cars on a boat.

Mar. 18. Some of the boys went out on the R.R. to work. I was not able. Bought some butter at 50 cts a lb.

Mar. 19. I visited an asylum in which was confined about 100 rebel prisoners. They looked rather wolfish.

Mar. 21. Georg Lazelere and myself visited the State House which is a splendid building. Saw many curiosities in the library and had a splendid view of the city from the top of dome.

Mar. 25. Col and men returned with one engine and 8 cars. In unloading the engine the boys proposing to work according to the pay received were grunting and tugging at it without moving it when one of the officers proposed they should give one $17.00 pull. It was done and the engine run off the boat without difficulty. A $13.00 lift wouldn't move it.

Mar. 28. John Forbes and John McDonald of Co C were arrested for refusing to do duty. A petition signed by nearly every man in the Co was handed to the Capt demanding our pay.

Apr. 1. We received orders to cook two days rations preparatory for marching. I was on guard.

Apr. 2. We rec'd orders to march at 10 A.M. Protests were drawn up in the various Co's and signed by the men refusing to go any farther unless paid our just dues. These were handed to the Col. Lieut [John W.] Williamson went and saw Gen [Ebenezer] Dumont, commanding the post. He said we must march and if we persisted in refusing, the leaders would be shot for mutiny, but said we should have an impartial hearing soon. The order to march was postponed one day. All who considered themselves unable to march and carry knapsacks were sent to the barracks. Capt Grant advised me to stay as I was weak, but I was ashamed to train in such a company and was one of but 36 left in the company who went through. We styled ourselves the undaunted few. I refused to sign the protest against marching but had all lived up to it I presume we would have all been discharged without pay.

Apr. 3. We left at 11 A.M. on the Nashville & Decatur R.R. We got within five miles of Columbia and marched in as a bridge was gone. Found Col Hunton and men there. The teams had not come yet so we had no tents to sleep in. Passed through a splendid country.

Apr. 4. Our entire regiment with the exception of Co's A & K (who were with Gen Mitchell) marched at 7 A.M. but a shower drove us in the County Fair Grounds for shelter. We made 12 1/2 miles through a fine country following in the wake of Buells army who had gone to Pittsburg Landing. Our teams came up late at night. I slept in a tent with Co. D.

Apr. 5. We made but 5 miles, a brigade being in advance of us and the roads very muddy. We camped in Summertown, a resort for hunters and the wealthy. We had plenty of fresh pork.

Apr. 6. We marched 13 miles carrying our knapsacks a part of the way on account of the bad roads, which were the worst I ever saw in my life. The country was poor and thinly inhabited.

Apr. 7. We went 15 miles over ridge roads which were good but a poor country. Rained all night. We could hear the cannonading of the Battle of Pittsburg Landing.

Apr. 8. We marched 12 miles over a rough country but well watered with springs. It rained all night.

Apr. 9. We went but 4 or 5 miles on account of bad roads.

Apr. 10. I was taken with a severe lameness in my knee and was compelled to fall in the rear. The reg't went off on a crossroad unbeknown to me, but I got in company with one Davis[3] in Co. C and we kept to the main road. Slept in a corn crib over night although the family wanted

3. Several soldiers with that surname were serving in Company C.

we should sleep in the house saying we might occupy the same bed Gen's Buell and Nelson did, but we preferred the corn crib. We loaded our guns to be ready for action.

Apr. 11. We plodded on again, my knee impeding my progress considerably. We went 5 miles and came to a mill where we staid over night sleeping in the bolter. In the morning we were covered with flour and looked more like millers than soldiers. I got some rations during the day of a commissary.

Apr. 12. We found the reg't encamped a mile from the river at Savannah. The Capt supposed me to be sick, lost or captured and was about to send someone back in search of me.

Apr. 13. I was detailed as cook for our tent. At 4 P.M. we received orders to march at 5 with one days cooked rations. We went to the river and slept on a barge loaded with bales of hay.

Apr. 14. The horses and wagons were loaded on some barges and towed up the river. We went up about 4. P.M. to the landing, marched two miles and went into camp on the battleground.

Apr. 15. We moved half a mile to a better camp ground.

Apr. 19. It rained all day and made our tent a perfect mud hole to stop in. The water was miserable. I looked around over the battlefield and see some of the dead that had been rolled up against a log and partially covered. Rails had been piled upon the horses and burned.

Apr. 20. Ser'g [Edwin] Osband and Corps [Charles] Vredenburg, [Joseph] Lake, [?] Brown, [David] Johnson, and [Frederic] McGee were reduced for signing the protest at Nashville, and [Albert] Vanderwarker was promoted Serg't and [George] Waldo, [Joseph] Braman, [Edd] Lapham, Wm Fullerton, and myself Corporals. I ranked as 8th Corp, but it finally paid as I got while Corp $20.00 per month.

Apr. 23. We drilled four hours for the first time since we left Camp Sorghum. Had skirmish drill and dress parade as 5 P.M.

Apr. 26. I was detailed to go to the river after rations etc.

Apr. 28. We rec'd an order for all the well men in Co's B, D, E, & H to go off to work taking three days rations and some tents. Our rations when off on such campaigns consisted of Hard tack, pork, and coffee, which was poor grub for laboring man. We went out seven miles and were set at building roads, bridges, etc. The reb's were but 1/2 mile ahead of us blocking up the roads by falling trees in them. We could hear them at work.

Apr. 29. Wood's & Thomas' Divisions passed us. The rest of our reg't came up.

May 1. I was on guard for the first time since leaving Nashville. At night we rec'd an order for all the well men to march in the morning as convalescents were substituted for guards in our places.

May 2. We marched at 10 A.M., the order being changed so as to include the whole of us. Went a round about way and camped on the direct Corinth road.

May 3. We went within six miles of Corinth repairing roads, etc. as we went along.

May 6. We left camp at 4 1/2 A.M. all who were able expected an attack would be made on Corinth. Had to build a bridge and wade around in water at various depths all of the time. We drew rations of whiskey at night. Made bough houses to sleep under to keep off the dew.

May 7. Were sent in advance of all but one picket post to build roads.

May 8. We started to take a rebel battery that had fired upon the Col but were ordered back.

May 9. We were sent to corduroy a swamp when our pickets were fired upon and driven in. The firing became brisk and we took out guns and formed on the right of some cavalry and some infantry on the left of them. The rebs charged the inf'try and cavalry who fled, which obligated us to retreat. Several of the infantry were killed and wounded. It was thought it would bring on a general engagement.[4]

May 11. Worked hard all day. Built us a splendid bough house to sleep in at night.

---

4. The Engineers under Innes suffered no loss and their conduct was praised. Officers of the other units involved were censured for leaving the field while the Engineer working parties remained.

May 17. Was a day of rest for us for the first time in two or three weeks.

May 18. Co's B & H reported to Gen Buell at 5 A.M. We were sent to the front to throw up a breastwork for four siege guns under Maj [Alvin] Gillem. There was skirmishing near us all day. A rebel shell burst near us. Our works were inspected by Gen's Buell, Pope, Nelson, McCook, Wood, & Crittenden.

May 20. It rained so we did not work. Amos Bradford[5] started for home carrying a great number of letters home for the boys.

May 21. Gov Blair arrived and left during the night without saying anything to us. He might have been mobbed had he not left as he did as the most bitter hatred was felt toward him by the men blaming him for not seeing wrongs adjusted.

May 28. While erecting some field hospitals I was ordered to arrest [Hiram] Cassler for refusing to obey Lt. [Harry J.] Chapel and take him before the Capt, which I did when the Capt waiting to know the truth of the story I told him and he released him. At night I had to arrest Ben Taylor for getting in a row with old [George] Onrod and marched him to the guard house. Some cannonading during the day.

May 29. We rec'd orders to pull up stakes as our water failed us. We went about a mile and encamped near a good spring. It was very warm.

May 30. I helped police the grounds. A story was started we were to report home the sixteenth of June. The rebs evacuated Corinth. We saw the smoke and heard the explosion of their magazine. Our troops soon moved, Nelson's command being the first to reach the town. Some prisoners were captured. We could hear the cars the night previous all night long.

---

5. A neighbor of the Kimballs who was probably visiting his son Bailey, a member of the Third Michigan Cavalry.

4

Bushwhackers
and Railroads

After the Confederate evacuation of Corinth, Union general Henry Halleck divided his forces into three main tasks: occupy northern Mississippi and repair supply routes in the rear; reinforce threatened points, including Arkansas; and send Buell eastward along the Memphis and Charleston Railroad through the Tennessee River Valley to Chattanooga, Tennessee. The eight companies of Michigan Engineers with him were part of Buell's command. En route they would connect up with two other companies of the regiment that had been attached to Brigadier General Ormsby Mitchel's forces, currently stationed along the captured railroad centered at Huntsville in northern Alabama.

The railroad line upon which Buell would depend for supply was in shambles. A two-company detachment of the Michigan Engineers and other troops from Mitchel's command operated about one hundred miles of the Memphis and Charleston Railroad between Decatur and Stevenson, but the major bridges and sections of track had been destroyed east and west of those points. The lines running back north to Nashville from Decatur and Stevenson were also largely destroyed. Buell's plan was to move his army along the railroad leading east from Corinth, making repairs along the way. Kimball and his comrades repaired Memphis and Charleston bridges as far eastward as Decatur in June and then most were shifted to make similar repairs to bridges on the Nashville and Decatur line throughout July.

Unlike in Kentucky, most civilians in the towns and countryside along this route were active supporters of the Confederacy, determined to slow the invaders. Two Michigan Engineers were ambushed by local guerillas just four days into their march from Corinth, and over the summer Kimball frequently noted attacks upon isolated Union working parties. Attacks quickly hardened the men's attitudes against neighboring civilians, who were believed to be involved in much of this guerilla warfare. Union troops struck back against the civilians, although official army policy still called for a hands-off treatment. Kimball's journal clearly demonstrates that gap between policy and practice.

During the summer the pay controversy continued to embroil the men in Kimball's regiment and he frequently wrote of it in his journal. The War Department ordered an investigation of Colonel Innes's conduct and he was cleared, though not without some criticism for how he handled the men. Overall, the report was very sympathetic to a valuable regiment of men who were laboring in vital tasks, yet not receiving the pay due them. Congress finally passed legislation in July to remedy the matter, officially establishing volunteer engineer regiments and setting the pay of engineer troops. It would still be months, however, before the War Department would get around to paying the regiment.

As Kimball and his comrades repaired the railroad, Confederate cavalry raids struck at the vulnerable track. By early August, however, Buell's supply line was reasonably intact back to Nashville and Louisville. The Michigan Engineers were ordered to Stevenson to construct wooden pontoon boats. These craft would be used in a forced crossing of the Tennessee River near Bridgeport, and then formed into a bridge for the passage of Buell's army toward Chattanooga.

Within two weeks, however, another Confederate cavalry raid shut down the Louisville and Nashville Railroad, with repairs projected to take weeks. More alarming, major Rebel forces were on the move in eastern Tennessee and Kentucky, threatening Buell's left flank and supply bases in Middle Tennessee. Buell began to withdraw his command from along the Tennessee River, moving back to Tennessee and then on to Kentucky when it appeared Rebel forces were driving on Louisville and the Ohio River. Kimball and his comrades in the Michigan Engineers were part of this rapid withdrawal of Buell's army back to

Louisville, arriving there in late September. Buell left forces behind to protect Nashville, and Kimball and others labored on the railroad as they worked their way north to Louisville.

June 1. Orders were rec'd for us to be ready to march at 8 A.M. We went to Corinth and then struck out on the Memphis and Charleston RR east carrying knapsacks. The day was very warm and Col Hunton, who was in command, marched us about eight miles without stopping to rest a moment. Some of the men were completely tired out when the Dr. rode up and told he must stop or he would kill all of the men.

June 2. We started early slinging our blankets over our shoulders. We found two bridges partially destroyed, which were soon repaired. We went nine miles and camped in Burnsville, a pleasant little town. The teams came up late and it was 10 o'clock before the tents were pitched.

June 3. We reached Iuka and ate dinner at the springs, which were very fine being of sulphur and mineral. It was as fine as a town as I saw in the south, the dwellings being large and tasty and everything wearing a clean and healthy appearance. It was afterward the scene of a severe battle. We went 13 miles and camped within a mile of Bear Creek. Old George was sun struck, but not seriously.

June 4. We were to fit up our camp in the forenoon and begin work on the bridge in the afternoon. Some of the men strayed off and two of Co. E's men went to the river when they were fired upon by bushwackers on the opposite side and one killed on the spot and the other wounded, but he reached camp and gave the alarm and the long roll beat at the same time Col Hunton was yelling to fall in or we would all be cut in pieces as the rebels were upon us. It created considerable excitement and one amusing incident. One of the boys in our Co who complained of being so lame he could not even get his food, when he heard the alarm jumped up and ran for the woods like a white head [very fast]. His brother also who boasted much of his courage showed unmistakable signs of uneasiness. We were soon in line and went down near the creek but came back a short distance and stopped in a ravine to await the advance of Gen Wood, but as he did not come we posted pickets and lay in the woods all night, our company acting as a reserve. They arrested some men who were going down the creek in a boat but they professed to be rebel soldiers who were sick of the war who had thrown away their arms and were going north.

June 5. Wood's division arrived. A part of our Co were sent after a flat boat down the creek and brought it some distance then tied it up and returned to camp.

June 6. Our entire Co was sent after the flat boat with a Co of Infty for guards. The current was pretty strong and the creek, which was a large one, was deep and we were obligated to be in the water much of the time. After working hard all day we finally reached the bridge. Had much sport.

June 7. Our Co started to guard our train to Eastport after rations, but infantry were sent and we returned. Dan Burr & I went in the country and got some cherries, berries and milked a couple of cows, which was the first milk I had since leaving Nashville. We run much risk taking no arms and the country was swarming with guerillas.

June 8. We went to work on the bridge and just as we reached there the body of Lt Col [James] Kirkpatrick of the 40th Ind was taken out of the water, he having been upset while crossing in a boat. He was in the water but a few moments but life was extinct. Gen [William S.] Smith was in camp to investigate in regard to our troubles. He gave us little satisfaction.

June 10. I rec'd three letters. J. D. Butler returned to the Co having went home from Ky on a 60 day furlough.

June 11. We raised three bents.[1] The paymaster arrived to pay us. At night we were called to the Capt's tent to sign the payroll, all refusing to do so but Old George.

June 12. Gen Smith addressed us advising us to take our pay at $13.00 per month. Some concluded to sign rolls. I did not. I sold my rations of

---

1. When constructing trestle bridges, the Michigan Engineers built vertical columns or "bents," each comprised of four lengths of timber braced in the middle and narrowing to a cap. The bents were then connected by horizontal braces and platforms to form the road or railroad bed of the bridge. During construction, the bents were very vulnerable to swift water and sudden floods.

whiskey for 50 cts. I had been some days saving it and it was my only means of supplying myself with Stamps and Paper.

June 13. Co's C, E, & H with the Col moved on. We marched 15 miles through a fine country. Camped near a good spring pitching no tents. Very warm.

June 14. Reached Tuscumbia by 10 A.M., a distance of 10 miles. We supposed we were to build the bridge there but moved on toward Decatur, camping two miles from Tuscumbia. Water scarce. I got a canteen full of molasses of the darkies. The 51st Ind Col [Abel] Streight, who was afterward captured near Rome, Ga. having been sent by Rosecrans from Murfreesboro, Tenn. to destroy the rebel and Foundries there. He afterward escaped from Libby Prison.

June 15. We took to the RR again as usual. Went through a fine country being the valley of the Tenn River. We reached Town Creek where the rebs had burned a bridge 300 ft in length. We camped 3/4 of a miles from the bridge in a fine shade but a long ways from water. Blackberries in abundance.

June 16. I was sent in the forenoon to load wood and sink a barrel in a spring near the bridge.

June 17. Went out in the woods to get out timber. I was set at carrying water for the choppers. I visited two splendid springs near each other and about a mile from the bridge. They were about 50 ft in diameter each and said to be unfathomable. The water looked like indigo water it was so blue, Owing perhaps to their depth.

June 20. I was sent out in the woods with a squad to get out timber. Didn't work very hard. On guard at night.

June 21. I got excused from work to wash and mend, also to write.

June 22. Worked on the bridge. At night someone proposed a game of euchre and we played several games before we realized it was sunday as we had been at work.

June 24. Several of us went in quest of some potatoes and got a pan full when a guard came and stopped us. A guard arrested Grosvenor but as we went with the Capt's consent, he was released. Had a shower the first since leaving Corinth. We attempted to get some milk in the morning but met with poor success.

June 25. Finished the bridge in the forenoon and in the afternoon moved to [Courtland], eight miles.

June 26. Ten of us from Co. H were detailed to push some truck cars with timber on them. The Col & Capt went with us. We went 14 miles and repaired one bridge. Had a heavy shower at night, our squad sleeping in a barn. We got a lot of potatoes with authority from Capt Grant.

June 27. We started with the cars about daylight. Reached Decatur, a distance of 8 miles, before breakfast. Eat at the Hotel. Victuals good but rather scant. The Col ordered the camp to be searched for potatoes. The officer in search found a sack in the Capt's tent the first thing. Col threatened to arrest him if he ever permitted any such thing again being done. Had a turkey for dinner. Blackberries without end, the bushes dropping to the ground.

June 29. Col Huntons teams came up but the men did not as Engine broke down that was hauling them. Had preaching by a Mr. [Lewis D.] Rhodes of Co. E.

June 30. The other Cos came up bringing us quite an amount of mail. They had to walk up the grades as the engine was such a poor one it could not haul the train loaded. Rec'd marching orders at night.

July 1. The paymaster left his safe in charge of Maj Hopkins and during the night it was stolen, although there was a guard placed over it. It was finally found in a mudhole nearby. It was a long mystery who stole it being evident that two must have done it as it was too heavy for one man to carry. A fellow in Co. G named [Edmund] Hayden on his deathbed in Nashville confessed being one of the number but would not reveal who his accomplice was. Maj Hopkins & Capt Grant each offered $20.00 for the recovery of it. Lt [Albert] Culver of Co E found it. We went to the ferry boat but it was out of order so we remained in Decatur over night. Had two pies.

July 2. I was on guard at night. Had ten men on my relief. The ferry boat was repaired so that we crossed during the afternoon and left on the cars about sundown for Huntsville. Passed a bridge where a train that Co. A were running was thrown down in a creek, the rebs having burned the stringers partly off when the train came on the bridge it went down. One of Co. A who was on the engine got caught so that the hot water was dripping on him, killing him by inches. He begged of the rebs to shoot him and end his suffering but they said let the D——Yankee die that way. Several were killed or captured.[2]

July 3. Pitched our tents in the forenoon and I strolled through town in the afternoon. It is a beautiful city watered by a spring which is one of the finest in the country. The water is forced into a large reservoir on a rise of ground and conducted from thence throughout the city.

July 4. Co's G & H left camp at daylight and took the cars to the junction of Nashville & Decatur RR and then proceeded to Elk River on the road, where we camped for the night and cooked up rations for the morrow. We had a blackberry shortcake for supper which was splendid. Altogether I enjoyed the anniversary of our independence very much.

July 5. We went to Pulaski, a very pretty little town and the county seat of Giles Co. Passed through a tunnel on the RR that was 80 rods in length and cut through solid rock and on a curve. It was very dark inside and we groped our way along as best we could. Several fell and bruised themselves. Bought me a straw hat, which was comfortable.

July 6. We went about seven miles and camped. Sold my overcoat for $2.00. One of the Co. G men got a bug in his ear during the night and set up a desperate howl. He got it out without much difficulty.

July 7. We set about rebuilding the bridge over Richland Creek that had been burned by the Rebs on their retreat from Nashville. We had just raised one bent when the coupling of a train above us broke and being heavy grade came toward us very fast. An alarm was given and we got off a proper distance. The cars came on and leaped over abutment, crushing our work and spoiling the cars that ran off which were two flat cars and a truck. Some of the boys got a spree. Came near having a row.

2. The incident occurred on May 1, 1862, when the bridge over Limestone Creek was set on fire and trains crewed by Michigan Engineers attempted to cross the burning span. Thomas Jenkinson of Company A died as Kimball describes and several others were injured. See Mark Hoffman, *My Brave Mechanics: The First Michigan Engineers and Their Civil War* (Detroit: Wayne State University Press, 2007), 74–75, for a more detailed account.

July 8. Mic Chamberlain, Newell [Slauson] & others came up.[3]

July 9. Co H went about three miles up track after timber.

July 10. Three of us went our foraging in the evening. Brought in a couple of fine ganders.

July 12. Joe Hawkins and myself bought some honey for the tent. Cotton is beginning to blossom.

July 13. We were allowed to rest but six of us went out after fruit, getting apples, peaches, etc. We had to stand picket at night. I had five men on my post.

July 14. We were excused from work. We bought 16 lbs of honey.

July 15. We had to go on picket again. Each squad had a canteen of whiskey.

July 17. We were called for to go on picket at 9 P.M. Twenty volunteers were wanted. I was one of the number. It stormed all day and during the night.

July 18. Capt Grant called us from picket and taking us to an old secesh by the name of Johnson, ordered our breakfast which was refused and taking forcible possession, ordered the slaves to get us the best the house offered. The pantry was locked and the old man refused to give up the key, so the capt broke open the doors. We had a splendid breakfast, the slaves telling us we would find the hams and I never saw a nicer in my life. We then had orders to take what we wished and we were going to make the old man take the oath of allegiance to which he objected when to scare him it was proposed we should hang him and procuring a rope it was placed about his neck, but he didn't scare worth a cent.

July 19. Heard cannonading in the direction of Murfreesboro. Moved our camp two miles to get out timber for the bridge. [Irving] Updike and [Irving] Thompson came from home. Co H was alone in the woods.

July 20. Vanderwarker and Chamberlain and myself went in the country after Negros to do the shopping for us. Took dinner with a

3. They had been left sick at Nashville when the regiment moved on. As Kimball frequently notes, men would be away from the regiment for months in rear-area hospitals.

planter. An alarm shot was fired and we were got in line. It amounted to nothing.

July 21. Was on picket having orders to fire on any one I saw approaching from the outside without challenging them. Had no occasion to fire.

July 22. A negro brought in his violin and the darkies did some dancing for us.

July 23. I had charge of a squad of negroes to chop. Loaded timber on the cars at night.

July 24. Twenty of our company went to a negro dance at night. Had a considerable sport. We had to keep a guard posted all the time. While here a somewhat amusing circumstance happened. One of our Co named [Hiram] Cassler had a felon on his hand and going out in the country a negress dressed it for him. Her master finding it out gave her a severe flogging for so doing which coming to the knowledge of the Capt Grant he disguised himself as a mule driver and with two others proceeded to his house and he acknowledged the act when the Capt told him they had come to settle with him for it and asking Geo Waldo what it was best to do with him, Waldo thought it best to pray and ask the Lord what should be done with him, which plan was adopted and Waldo, who was a very profane man, kneeled down and prayed. When he said the Lord had answered his prayer and said whip him so they ordered him to take off his coat and gave him a flogging with a mule whip. Finally the Capt asked Waldo what it was best to do with him and Waldo said it was best to pray, which he did, receiving an answer that the Lord said whip him and they proceeded to chastise again. They finally made him beg and promise to never do so again, and compelling him to take the oath of allegiance they left him.

July 25. We joined Co G at the second bridge below the station, moving on the cars.

July 26. Was on guard the night before and went as guard for our team foraging. Got two geese, etc.

July 27. Worked in the forenoon. Visited a plantation and had quite a discussion with the ladies who avered we never could conquer the South and advised us to go home immediately.

Aug. 1. We finished the bridge the day before, but a train passing over cracked a stringer which compelled us to put in another bent. We expected to go to Elk River on the cars so our teams, tents, etc., were sent ahead leaving us without grub.

Aug. 2. We pressed a team to carry our knapsacks and started on the march. Pressed our dinners of the niggers through mistake some of them killing chickens and cooking them with their heads on and a portion of their entrails left in. It was hard to relish. Marched as far as Richland Creek where we gave orders for our breakfast. A dead mule lay by the side of the road thoroughly rotten and in order to pass it we took a long breath and double quicked past it.

Aug. 3. Arrived at Elk River in time to see the first train pass safely over it. An attack was expected at night. The 6th Ky went through the manual of arms on parade and were splendidly drilled. Col. [Walter] Whittaker commanding.

Aug. 4. A guerilla was brought in a rope put around his neck ordering him to expose the gang which he did. The 6th Ky killed three of them. We took the cars for Huntsville, arriving about 8 P.M.

Aug. 5. Went to Stevenson where we found Co's A, B & K.

Aug. 6. The whole reg't was together for the first time since leaving Louisville.

Aug. 7. I got a pass for 20 of us to go in a swimming. It had to be countersigned by the Provost Marshall.

Aug. 9. We had dress parade for the first time in the South.

Aug. 10. We had inspection at 9 A.M. standing in the hot sun for about two hours. On dress parade, owing to a change of officers, the Co's assumed different positions, Co H taking the place of Co. F.

Aug. 13. Mic and myself sent home a box of stuff by express. Began pontoons in the afternoon.

Aug. 14. Was on guard taking the first relief. Cap Grant returned from Nashville, having gone there for some of the boys. Chas Fowler and myself went out foraging, got some peaches. Several of the boys came up from Nashville.

Aug. 15. We worked on the pontoons. The sutler brought in some beer and officers and men had a spree. Serg't Shumway started for Mich to recruit men.

Aug. 16. We elected the balance of our noncommissioned officers. J. P Lapham 5th Serg't, Ephraim Fullerton 4th Corp, Chas Hoyer 7th Corp, and A. D. Welling 8th Corp. [William B.] Conley of Co A drew a sketch of our pontoon building.

Aug. 17. Worked on the pontoons and had inspection at 4 P.M. Two of our men were captured by the rebs while working in a saw mill. Co A followed them to the Tenn River.[4]

Aug. 18. We were mustered by order of the President. Capt Grant returned having gone after Glover, but finding him wounded left him. He was shot while carrying dispatches for some general.[5]

Aug. 21. Co. H went to the Tenn River foraging when we saw the rebel pickets on the opposite bank. Several of our reg't were courtmartialled and their sentence read on dress parade.

Aug. 22. We were routed at 3 A.M. and were loaded on the cars at 10 A.M., arriving at Nashville at 10 P.M. the country is very rough from Stevenson to Decherd.

Aug. 23. We remained in Nashville until near night—when we went out 12 miles on the L&N RR.

Aug. 24. I helped to unload the cars and had a fine swim in the Cumberland River. Bob Hill and Chas Mingo of Co A were kept tied all day and night the first for getting drunk and the other for staying in Nashville.

Aug. 25. Co. H was detailed to do the picket duty while the other Co's did the work.

4. They were working at Jackson's Mill near Stevenson. Benjamin R. Rice of Company I and Daniel W. Moore of Company A were paroled after their capture and sent north for formal exchange. The runaway slaves working alongside them were undoubtedly returned to their owners or killed.

5. Samuel S. Glover of Company H was shot in the thigh on July 13 near Fayetteville, Tennessee, while carrying dispatches to Buell's headquarters. He was discharged by the surgeon on account of the wounds, which still bothered him decades later.

Aug. 26. We built us a bough house. Raccoons are plenty, coming very near us at night.

Aug. 27. We were relieved from guard duty by the 9th Ind.

Aug. 28. Our negro, Carter, died of Typhoid Fever.

Aug. 29. We worked on the bridge. A fellow in Co D died suddenly.

Aug 31. Worked as usual. I was on guard duty at night. An alarm shot was fired and the men got in line. It proved to be some of our own cavalry who did not hear the challenge of the picket and were fired upon when they returned the fire. No one was hurt. Had a heavy shower while at work. All got soaked.

Sept. 1. The weather was much cooler. The report of the battle of Bulls Run was received by telegraph.[6]

Sept. 2. Mic and myself went out minus a pass getting our dinners and some apples. Weather chilly.

Sept. 3. We broke camp about noon. Ten from each Co were detailed as wagon guard. I was one of the number. Went about 5 miles; the 9th Ind & 27th Ky were with us.

Sept. 4. We went about four miles farther and stopped where another bridge had been burned.

Sept. 5. We went at work at the bridge. Lieut Grant read an order that we were to receive what we enlisted for. We gave three cheers.

Sept. 6. The bridge was over Pilot Knob Creek. We had to sleep on our arms.

Sept. 7. Nearly finished the bridge. Expected an attack from the rebs. Woods division came up.

Sept. 8. We marched at 4 A.M. reaching Gallatin by sunrise. We tramped until night without our dinners, camping near Mitchelville. This was the commencement of the hardest marching we did in the service. Gen Jno Morgan of the rebel army lay near the road where we passed and saw us pass without molesting us as he supposed we were

---

6. The Union defeat in the second battle of Bull Run in Virginia.

the advance of Buell's army. He had 4,000 or 5,000 men with him and we about that many hundred. They lay near enough to read the name of our reg't upon our wagons, yet was unseen by us. This report came from some of his men who were captured.

Sept. 9. We started before sunrise, stopping at Franklin until night and then marched all night, resting about two hours near morning, and then pushed on to Bowling Green, arriving at 8 A.M. Will Gavett and myself captured a horse which we traded with Lieut Grant and after riding him alternately for a while, sold him for $10.00. Our Co. acted as rear guard, a great many of the men tired out and got on the wagons to ride. Several Horses and Mules dropped dead from the heat.

Sept. 10. We slept all day and night. Had a thorough wash.

Sept. 12. I helped repair the pontoon bridge. Wrote a letter home for the first time in over a month.

Sept. 13. Fifteen of the best men from each Co were detailed to work on the fort on College Hill. Built platforms for the cannon.

Sept. 14. A man came and claimed Lieut Grant's horse and took him away. Two men were drowned in the river.

Sept. 16. I was at the river and saw one of the men that was drowned. He was brought to the surface by firing cannon across the river. We rec'd orders to march at 3 P.M., leaving the sick, tents, knapsacks, etc., behind. We were divided in three divisions, Co's A, C, & H under Major Hopkins composing ours. We went with Gen Rousseau about five miles and camped.

Sept. 17. We started again at daylight and marched 18 miles, suffering much for want of water. It rained at night. Mic and myself got a cup of butter and canteen of milk and then crawled in a corn crib which kept us dry, but we slept cold as the wagons did not come up, so I was without coat or blanket. Capt Grant was unwell and returned to Bowling Green.

Sept. 18. We had orders to cook up three days rations but had to march before finishing. We camped near Pruetts Knob with about 50,000 other troops. It was quite late when we got in and I never saw a finer sight as their camp fires were all burning brightly, rails being used for firewood. It was clear and cold. The teams did not come up so we had no covering but the sky.

Sept. 19. We were routed out by daylight and waited for our teams to come up. 4,100 paroled federal prisoners passed us who were captured at Green River. We went 3 or 4 miles and camped. The 10th Wis captured 30 rebels and killed two.

Sept. 20. Rested all day. [Benton] Green of Co C shot a horse accidentally.

Sept. 21. We started before daylight with one brigade under [Gen. Lovell] Rousseau and some cavalry and marched 17 miles to reach Glasgow, 8 miles distant, expecting to intercept Gen [John C.] Breckinridge's ammunition train and capture it. Found three hospitals filled with sick rebels. Maj Hopkins was riding by us and we were pushing right along when Cassler accosted him with (Major a little faster if you think your horse can stand it). The night was chilly and no blankets. We started with but one days rations.

Sept. 22. We started for Glasgow before daybreak for Munfordsville. The day was hot and no rations. Rob Freeman and myself got our dinners at a house. He was going to charge us but 5 cts a piece, but we gave him 25 cts. Forded Green River at night and camped on the back. No tents, blankets, or food. The officers bought a few shoulders and hardtack for us. The shoulders were full of maggots but they were eaten. Had a scare. At night, some horses running away. Some of the boys hurt themselves in the dark.

Sept. 23. We started at 8 A.M. and stopped at Bacon Creek for dinner. Went on to Nolin Creek, getting there at midnight. The boys were hard up but eight on Co. H being present to stack arms. I was one of the number. The teams came up with eight blankets.

Sept. 24. We started at daylight, taking the advance most of the way. Marched 23 miles. Had our blankets and plenty of grub so we were happy.

Sept. 25. Marched to West Point and rep'd the pontoon bridge over the Salt River. Mic and I went down on board a steamer and as we were returning we saw Capt of the 6th [Ohio] get badly whipped by a mule driver for interfering with his team. Saw my cousin Henry Kimball in an Ohio reg't.[7]

Sept. 26. We took the steamer *Poland* about noon and went to Portland from which place we marched to the suburbs of Louisville, where we camped. Had a splendid ride up the river.

Sept. 27. It rained all day. We slept in an old house. We rec'd some new recruits. Ben Whinney [Winne] came up for the first time since he left us at Camp Wickliff.

Sept. 28. Gen Nelson was shot at the Galt House by Gen Jeff C. Davis.[8] We sold our surplus coffee for $10.00 20 cents apiece. Some of the boys got tight. George Waldo was one of the number. I had to arrest him and told a lie to get him clear.

Sept. 29. Gen Nelson was buried, Charley Fowler and myself attending without a pass, but we were not arrested. He was a very large man, his coffin filing the hearse. His favorite horse followed, the horse saddled and equipped for mounting with his boots with spurs attached in the stirrups and draped in mourning. Many prominent officers followed him to the grave. I shed no tears over his death though he was a good fighting general but very tyrannical and abusive if everything was not done up right, but if everything was done in a manner to please him no one could be more condescending. When we first reached Camp Wickliffe a live general was quite a sight and some of the boys stood staring at him when he asked them what the hell they were looking at him for in a voice and manner that started them to their quarters in a hurry.

7. First cousin Henry Kimball was a member of Company D, Thirty-eighth Ohio and survived his three-year enlistment. Henry's older brother William died in May 1862 serving in the same company.

8. Brigadier General Jefferson C. Davis. Drawing upon his military record and political connections, perhaps along with sympathy from others in high ranks who had been abused by the volatile Nelson, Davis was quickly restored to his command.

5

"My Brave Mechanics"

OCTOBER 1–DECEMBER 29, 1862

By late September, General Buell and most of his army were together in Louisville, recovering from the hurried march north. He reorganized his forces for the upcoming campaign to drive the Confederates from Kentucky. As before, the Michigan Engineers were split into detachments and assigned to the various columns. Major Hopkins with Companies A, C, and H was assigned to General Alexander M. McCook's I Corp. Colonel Innes with four companies joined with General Thomas L. Crittenden's II Corps. Lieutenant Colonel Hunton and the three remaining companies were attached to a special small diversionary column under Brigadier General Joshua Sill. General Charles Gilbert's III Corps did not have any Michigan Engineers attached.

Buell's targets were the two major Confederate forces operating in Kentucky, the Army of Mississippi command by Bragg and Major General E. Kirby Smith's smaller independent command. Bragg and Smith were confused by the various Union marching columns and which one posed the greatest threat. During the first week of October, marching Union columns moved steadily closer to the enemy, which remained scattered and more focused on the installation of a Confederate governor at the state capital at Frankfort than the movement of Buell's army.

Kimball and the balance of Hopkins's battalion moved from Louisville through Taylorsville and Chaplinville. Their march was made during a period of prolonged drought, and the hot dusty columns of both sides suffered greatly from the lack of potable water. On the night of October 7, Hopkins's battalion settled into camp at Mackville, under orders to continue the march early in the morning toward Perryville where Buell's forces were converging. They made camp amid the sounds of distant artillery fire as Gilbert's forces probed against the enemy on the outskirts of Perryville.

By this point, most of Bragg's forces were also gathering in the Perryville area, and he was determined to attack what he thought was only a portion of Buell's command. He arrived in person to take direct command early on October 8, intending to use a wide flanking attack on his right to strike the enemy and roll up its left flank brigade by brigade moving north to south.

As they arrived at Perryville late in the morning of the 8th, McCook's divisions were posted on the Union left; Kimball and his comrades in Hopkins's battalion were assigned a position in the rear, supporting Simmons's Indiana battery. Not realizing the extent of the Union line, Bragg launched an attack around what he thought was an area devoid of Union troops. Both sides were surprised to discover each other, as the Confederates had expected no resistance, and the Union defenders had thought they faced only enemy cavalry. Bragg's forces had the momentum and numbers and steadily drove the Union forces back. The surviving Perryville accounts from men in Hopkins's battalion vary in details but are consistent in recounting a shifting role from battery support for the Fifth Indiana Battery into hard fighting as infantry alongside Loomis's Michigan Battery while Confederate forces drove most of the left flank from the field.

Some Union regiments gave ground slowly while many of the new regiments broke quickly. By 4:30 P.M. what remained of the forces on the Union left had been driven back to a position among the buildings and fences of the Russell farm, near the intersection of the Benton and Mackville roads. Union commanders desperately sought any available troops while they awaited the shift of reinforcements from the Union center and right.

Hopkins and his three companies of the Michigan Engineers were among those thrown into the fight during this last desperate effort. One of the men wrote home that the major led the three companies into battle with the cry, "Now my brave mechanics if you can work you can

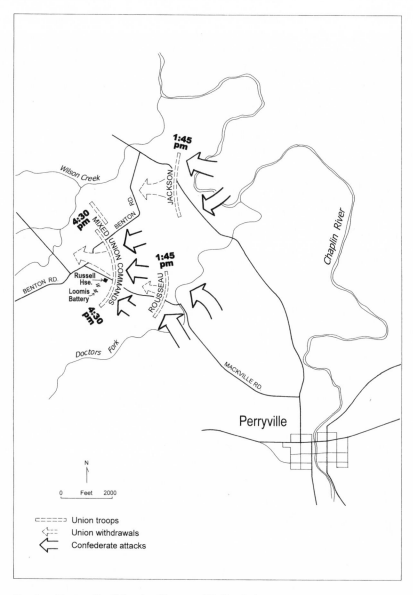

Battle of Perryville. (Map by Sherman Hollander)

fight, follow me."[1] It was a hard but short fight, and the Engineers fell back from the Russell farm position soon after with the rest of the overwhelmed Union line. The Confederate advance was brought to a halt by late-arriving Union reinforcements and darkness. Because of the nature of the fighting and collapse of the Union left, there was great confusion as officers sought to reassemble the remnants of their commands for the likely resumption of fighting in the morning. Kimball's account of his wanderings that night paints a vivid picture of the confusion.

Dawn came with Kimball and others fully expecting a continuation of the fight, but Bragg's forces were in retreat. He had finally realized that he faced virtually all of Buell's army and withdrew to join with Kirby Smith's command. Buell's forces followed belatedly, and within a week the Confederates were on their way out of Kentucky and back to Tennessee. Buell, too, was soon gone, replaced for his poor performance at Perryville.

Hopkins and his men were reunited with the other detachments of Michigan Engineers and were back in Bowling Green by the end of the month. For the rest of 1862, the men worked to repair Union supply lines leading to and around Nashville. Major General William Rosecrans assumed command of what was now being referred to as the Army of the Cumberland. He was under strict orders from Washington to move quickly against Bragg's forces, which were now in position near Murfreesboro, south of Nashville.

The Michigan Engineers had a critical role in getting Rosecrans's supply line back in order, but their work was great hampered by renewed arguments in the regiment over the pay issue. On November 10, more than one hundred of the men from five companies refused to march, and they were arrested and taken to Nashville. Though only one man in Kimball's Company H refused to march that day, the patience of the others was running out. Kimball and several others held firm twelve days later when again ordered to march and were arrested. They remained with the regiment but were reduced in rank before taking the oath of allegiance and being returned to their companies.

The pay issue was eventually resolved and the Michigan Engineers received their pay as volunteer engineers on December 8. Those who had mutinied on November 10 were tried in Nashville—most were convicted,

---

1. James M. Sligh to James W. Sligh, October 17, 1862, Sligh Family Papers, Bentley Historical Library, University of Michigan, Ann Arbor.

reduced in rank with a loss in pay, and were not released until late January. Kimball notes their return on February 2, 1863.

The rest of December was spent in various work details, receiving new equipment, and drilling. In general, the work was light and the food better than it had been for months.

Oct. 1. We marched at daylight, passing through Jeffersontown and camped near Fisherville, maybe 16 or 17 miles.

Oct. 2. We went to Taylorville, 15 miles, rained during the day and night. I slept in a barn. We drew new clothing at Louisville so we had the appearance of new troops. Some soldiers came along and began to deride us when we inquired how long they had been in the service. They said six months. They left when we told them we had seen a years service.

Oct. 4. We moved to within a mile of Bloomfield.

Oct. 5. We remained in camp all day. Two sutlers opened up their goods for sale. The boys having no money stole what they could. Was on guard at night.

Oct. 6. We marched to Chaplinville, then down a ravine and crossing the Chaplin river, camped.

Oct. 7. Marched to Maxville, where we heard cannonading all night at intervals and we very well knew there were rebels in the vicinity and the probabilities were we would have a chance at them.

Oct. 8. We marched about 11 miles, a considerable [part] of the way on the double quick. Cannons were firing all the time. Gen Rousseau came along and told us we would take a hand before night. We reached the battlefield and formed in line of battle. We were placed in support of an Ind battery where we remained until afternoon when Gen McCook gave the Maj orders to pile up our blankets and go in. We fought until dark supporting Loomis battery toward the last. Just at dark some infantry falling back broke us all up. I remained until the firing had ceased, when, in company with one of Co. A, we started to look for some water, being thirsty and tired. We were fired upon once by some unknown person but were too tired to make any effort to find out. At last we came to a mud-hole with soldiers as thick as bees around a hive and so thick was the mud and water that we sucked the water between our teeth. We concluded to lie down near the spring and in the night get up and fill our canteens so we cut a lot of green broom corn growing near and as the rebels drove us back and got our blankets we had no covering and it was very chilly. We had not lain long when I heard the familiar voice of Mic Chamberlain and Doc Walker at the spring. We occupied the greater part of the night telling our experience and who we saw wounded, etc. The stock of my gun rec'd a rebel ball that otherwise could have hit me.

Oct. 9. We made us some coffee in the morning and finding a tree loaded with hickory nuts we made a meal of them. Mic and I entered a deserted house and found a little corn bread and a small canister of tea which we appropriated to our own use. We took a stroll over the battle field and then joined the company. The dead were all left for the citizens to bury.

Oct. 10. We moved 2 or 3 miles and drew up in line expecting another battle. It rained and was quite cold.

Oct. 11. The Col's division joined us. We went 2 or 3 miles and camped on the pike.

Oct. 12. I was detailed as wagon guard. Went 8 miles.

Oct. 13. Went with the wagons. Sutler opened, trusting us.

Oct. 14. We passed through Danville, went 15 miles.

Oct. 15. Saw the 4th Mich Cav. Capt Grant came up. At night Cap Grant told us to secure some straw to sleep on from a stack nearby. I went to get some for Mic and I when there were so many there I found it impossible and going in the barn saw some bundles of rye unthreshed and appropriated some of it for my own use. One of McCooks staff riding by saw me lugging them to camp and asked me what I had there. I told him straw. He rode up alongside and felt of the heads. He asked me what reg't I belonged and who authorized me to get it. I told him my officers did. He doubted it and ordered me to take the bundles up to Col Innes headqrs with him. I hesitated some but started on slowly. He got a couple of rods ahead and looking back he as he passed through the gap in the field saw me coming all right and ordered me to hurry up and rode on. I thought it my opportunity then and dropping the bundles struck out down the road lively. I soon jumped the fence and dodging behind some old sheds saw no more of him. I told Mic what had happened and he went for straw while I kept out of sight, supposing they would search the camp, but I heard no more from it.

Oct. 16. We remained in camp baking up our flour, etc. Were divided in coffee pot squads. Had to get up during the night to warm. Quite frosty.

Oct. 19. We were hard up for provisions, grating up corn for pancakes. Rec'd three days rations at night. Put up tents for the first time since leaving Louisville.

Oct. 20. Marched at 4 ½ A.M. taking the Lebanon pike at Stanford. Camped near a farm owned by Rev. Dr. Breckinridge in a splendid country. Went 20 miles.

Oct. 21. Went 15 miles through a rough country and camped on the rolling fork. I bought some butter of a lady and she asked me where I was from. I told her from Mich. In all honesty she wanted to know what part of Ky Mich was in.

Oct. 22. Passed through Lebanon where we took dinner and camped on the Rolling Fork. Distance between 20 & 25 miles.

Oct. 23. Remained at camp all day drawing clothing, etc. Sutler opened a new stock of goods.

Oct. 24. Rec'd marching orders at noon. Went to Saloma.

Oct. 25. Took the Nashville road. Snowed two inches at night.

Oct. 26. Remained in camp all day. Some of the boys got turkeys, chickens, etc. Our knapsacks were distributed. Very Cold.

Oct. 27. Crossed Green River & Little Barren, camping on the latter. Carried knapsacks. Got a few chestnuts.

Oct. 28. We marched 14 miles in the forenoon and camped where we had passed but a month before. Mic and I got our dinners at a private house. It was quite a treat to eat at a table again.

Oct. 29. Marched 18 or 20 miles and camped within three miles of Dripping Springs. Carried knapsacks.

Oct. 30. We camped within nine miles of bowling green. I found a lot of persimmons, had quite a feast. Giles Noble had a heart attack of bilious colic. Doc Walker stuffed him with Davis painkiller, giving it to him by the spoon full. It was quite amusing.[2]

Oct. 31. We passed through Bowling Green and camped at the Sinking Creek with Gen Sills division. Sinking Creek was quite a curiosity being in a deep ravine, the water rushing out from the rocks and running rapidly a few rods, hides itself again, but empties in the river a few miles below. I stood on a rock where tradition has it Daniel Boone shot an Indian. There had been an old mill once in the ravine run by the water it being rapid and abundant enough to need no dam. Some of the boys attempted to explore the cavern below but could not proceed far.

Nov. 1. I was on detail policing the grounds, etc.

Nov. 2. Had regimental inspection at 9 A.M. Were again divided in four tents, separating Mic and I.

Nov. 3. Had charge of the guards at Sill's Hdqtrs. He was killed at Stone River and diminutive in stature.

Nov. 4. Marched at daylight, our reg't in advance. Went 22 miles, camping 4 miles south of Franklin.

Nov. 5. Started again at daylight, Co's A & H having the van, then a section of artillery. Camped at Tyree Springs, a summer resort for the wealthy.

Nov. 6. Marched in the same order as before to within 7 miles of Nashville, camping near a church.

Nov. 7. Mic and I started after some persimmons when I picked up a pocket book containing $16.00. Let Mic have $5.00. Several houses were burned near the camp before leaving. We went to Edgefield.

---

2. Colic with an accumulation of bile in the intestines. "Perry Davis' Vegetable Pain Killer" was patented in 1845 and widely used for pain. Its ingredients included opiates and ethyl alcohol.

Nov. 9. Henry House who was reported as having died, joined us. We had to have a pass to go after water even. The Col & Qm Masters wives are here.

Nov. 10. We were to march at 7 A.M. Co I and a portion of most of the other Co's refused to march unless paid as they enlisted. They were arrested and taken charge of by the Provost Marshall. Joe Lake was the only one from our company.

Nov. 11. We began work on the Manscove Creek bridge. Co H had all the guard duty to perform. Heme Grant[3] came quite sick. It rained all night.

Nov. 13. Finished the bridge. Bought a lot of chickens and stole a lot of honey so that the Co feasted.

Nov. 14. Marched at daylight. Co's A, B, C, & D went with Col Hunton, the balance with the Maj. We stopped near Hendersonville and began work on a bridge there.

Nov. 16. Put up the bents in the forenoon. Some of the boys went out at night and got chickens, mutton, and honey. Rec'd a considerable mail.

Nov. 17. Finished the bridge. I was on guard posting one in an ambulance and one under a wagon. It rained.

Nov. 19. We went to our old camp ground in Edgefield. Col Huntons command marched from Pilot Knob.

Nov. 20. We carried up some rails for wood when the Col ordered them all carried back. We voided it by cutting them in two. The Orderly Serg't of Co F came over from Nashville after their mail with a Provost Guard. The orderly was tied to a tree and the guard put in the guard house. Some more guards came and released both. The men cheered considerably.

Nov. 22. We were ordered to strike tents and march at 7 A.M. It was the understanding that nearly the entire reg't should bolt. They had to

3. Probably Heman D. Grant, brother of Captain Marcus Grant and a member of the Fourth Michigan Cavalry

make a detail to strike the tents. The Col swore we would all be shot if we did not march for mutiny. Thereby scaring all but 15 of Co H & 8 of Co A into marching. The names of those in Co H who refused to march were Serg't J. P. Lapham, Corps G. W. Green, Wm. H Kimball, Chas Hoyer, Geo Bachler, Wm. Ingalls, Wm Herrick, Josiah Easton, James Lahr, Fred McGee, James Lyon, R. B. Swift, Wm Simpson, B. T. Taylor, A. J. Walker. We expected to go across the river with the other boys, but were arrested by our own request and placed in the rear of our Co's and marched with our knapsacks on. We were all reduced to second class privates. Marched to Mill Creek, 8 miles, and had to police the grounds. Put up a couple of tents for ourselves.

Nov. 23. Were well fed and did some choring with knapsacks on. We stuffed them with straw to make them light. Capt Grant said by signing a confession we might return, which we did after some discussion.

Nov. 24. Had a very easy time. Would call for a guard every time we wanted anything. Lieut. Chapel went to Nashville to attend the trial of the boys.

Nov. 25. We were taken before Col Hunton one at a time and he administered the oath of allegiance to us when we were sent to our Co's.

Nov. 26. The bridge was finished in the forenoon and in the afternoon six of us went foraging, got our dinners only. Our reduction was read to the co.

Nov. 28. We rec'd a box from Sandstone containing dried fruit, butter, etc. Hattie Fuller sent us a small cheese.

Nov. 29. Sills division camped near us. We had a splendid meal of Biscuit, butter, cheese, stewed fruit, etc.

Nov. 30. I was on guard. It rained all day and very hard at night. The worst night in fact I ever stood on guard. Slept with Bill Brown in his wagon, as he drove Co. team.

Dec. 1. My birthday but rec'd no presents. We signed the pay and clothing rolls.

Dec. 5. It was cold and snowy. Froze hard at night. I slept cold. Worked at the tool tent during the day.

It is unclear when this wartime photo of Kimball was taken, but it was probably in either December 1862 or March 1864 in Nashville. Kimball references sitting for images on both occasions and he is not wearing the original uniform issued in 1861. (Collection of Max Miller)

Dec. 6. We have four roll calls a day to keep the men from going out of camp. Very cold at night.

Dec. 8. I was on detail to cut wood and while so doing the paymaster came in an ambulance escorted by some cavalry. Co H was paid. I rec'd $170.45, being $13.00 per month until promoted Corp and then $20.00 We were paid from enlistment to the 1st Sept. They deducted Walt Kimballs Sutler acc't which was rectified.[4]

Dec. 9. Most of the Co had a spree. Serg't Young started for Michigan recruiting. I sent $100.00 by him and $20.00 by mail.

Dec. 10. Went to Nashville with 9 others, saw Reuben Grant and sent $60.00 home by him. Had some photos taken. My dinner cost me $1.00. We were to be back by 4 P.M. but were 20 minutes late.

---

4. Apparently William Kimball was assigned responsibility for Walter Kimball's account with the sutler. The relationship between William and Walter Kimball, also of Jackson County and Company H, is unclear. The latter had been discharged because of wounds received in battle at Perryville.

Dec. 11. We drew soap for the first time in two weeks having made soft soap to use. Drew a blanket.

Dec. 12. Moved camp a mile nearer town on the Nolinville pike. Was on guard and had to remain in the old camp until dark.

Dec. 14. Had inspection. My gun was praised considerably.

Dec. 15. Stormed very hard all night. Our tent leaked very bad. Drew five conical stoves to the company.

Dec. 16. We were all set at work making ax handles.

Dec. 19. I was detailed to chop wood thereby avoiding squad drill. Dress parade at night. Rec'd three letters.

Dec. 20. Started at 4 A.M. for Manscove Creek foraging. Staid overnight having scant rations.

Dec. 21. Started for camp filling up the wagon as we went along. Reached camp just as the reg't was on parade. The order of exercises are roll call, 6 A.M.; sick call, 7:30; guard mounting 8; non commish drill 9 to 2 P.M.; Co drill 3 to 4; Dress parade & roll call, 4; Supper at 5; Tattoo roll call at 7; taps, 7:30. Patching it on pretty thick.

Dec. 25. Sutler brought a lot of fresh oysters & butter and we had a Merry Christmas.

Dec. 26. Stormed nearly all day. Co's A & H had a mock fight with oyster cans. Had a mock fight among ourselves making much sport.

Dec. 27. Marched at 7:30 with axes, leaving 12 men to strike tents. Camped on Mill Creek pike. Got out RR ties. Nigger John was hung near our camp.[5]

Dec. 28. Went about six miles on the Nolinville pike and built a bridge the rebels had a torn down with picks. Carried our guns and accoutrements and an axe. The right-wing returned to camp.

Dec. 29. Our Co had to get out 126 ties, 4 to a man. All had to wash their clothes and bodies. Cassler was going to refuse when the Capt gave orders for the men to scrub him if he did not. He complied.

---

5. Identity not clear, but Kimball notes on January 12 that the man had not been killed and was back with the regiment.

6

Lavergne

December 30–March 19, 1863

In late December, Rosecrans moved his army forward and prepared to battle Bragg's Confederates in their positions outside of Murfreesboro, along Stones River. Both commanders intended the same tactic—a preemptive strike with their left flank against the enemy, but the Confederates struck first on the morning of December 31. Rosecrans's right flank was driven back almost ninety degrees to a position along the Nashville to Murfreesboro pike. The Confederate success had come at a price, and Bragg did not renew the attack on January 1, believing Rosecrans would be forced to retreat. Rosecrans, however, held his ground and inflicted heavy losses when the Confederates renewed the fighting on January 2 with an attempt on the other Union flank.

In late December, Bragg had sent his cavalry deep into the Union rear to cut the flow of reinforcements and supplies between Nashville and Buell's army. Fearing such a tactic, Rosecrans had stationed several units along the Nashville Pike, including the Michigan Engineers. Innes moved his command to near the village of Lavergne on December 31, where they found the smoking remnants of one destroyed wagon train and were discouraged by the steady flow of Union wounded and stragglers falling back from the hard fighting near Murfreesboro. The Michigan Engineers took position on a hill near the pike and prepared a hurried defensive position of wagons and brush.

On January 1, Innes sent scouting parties into the surrounding countryside to give word of approaching Confederate cavalry. Kimball was on one of these patrols, along with Captain Grant and two others from the company. The four of them were almost cut off by enemy cavalry, escaping only by putting spurs to their horses, and they reached the regiment to find it preparing for a hard fight.

The Confederate cavalry was led by Brigadier General John A. Wharton and included about twelve hundred men with two pieces of light artillery. They were part of a larger force under Brigadier General Joseph Wheeler that was ranging up and down the pike destroying wagons and cutting up parties of Union soldiers. Innes had only about four hundred men, but they repulsed repeated attacks by Wharton and endured artillery fire, to which they couldn't reply. The many colorful accounts vary in detail but consistently point to a determined defense of the wagon and brush position. Innes refused several demands to surrender, and Wharton eventually withdrew his men for easier pickings elsewhere.

Though a small fight, Lavergne was a major victory for the morale of the army and the nation, especially when it became clear how close Rosecrans's army had been to destruction. It was also the event most associated with the Engineers during their four years of service, and Kimball provides us with a detailed account. Victory came at a cost. Three of Kimball's comrades were killed or mortally wounded, another four too seriously wounded for further service, and several others were captured. Wharton probably lost close to fifty killed, wounded, or captured.

After several days on alert, Kimball and his comrades went back to work repairing the roads and railroad leading from Nashville to Rosecrans's battered forces at Murfreesboro. That completed, they moved back to near Nashville by the middle of February and were shuttled to and from various railroad repair projects, especially the Nashville and Decatur Railroad bridge at Franklin. By the middle of March, their work was nearing completion, and the regiment received orders to march to Murfreesboro for work at that post.

Dec. 30. Col Innes came from Nashville at 10 P.M. and reported 5,000 rebel cavalry within four miles of us where they had burned a wagon train for us. We were called up to draw our wagons in a hollow square, after which we retired sleeping on our arms.

Dec. 31. We were in line at 4 A.M. and after standing in line awhile and sending the bugler around in different places to blow the reveilee so as to make it appear we had a large force, we stuck tents and prepared to march at 7. Went to Lavergne and having no further orders we stopped in a cedar grove nearby. Several houses were on fire and wagons that had been fired by the rebels the night before. It was reported the rebel cavalry were on our old camp ground shortly after we left it, but did not follow us.

Jan 1. This was one of the most eventful and trying days of service. In the morning some rude breastworks were thrown up of logs and brush and in the afternoon Col Innes told Capt Grant to take two or three of his men and scout the country as far as the Nolinville pike and learn if there were any rebel cavalry lurking about as reported. Serg't Vanderwarker, Joe Hawkins and myself were chosen to accompany him. I was enjoying a game of euchre at the time but postponed it. We were well mounted. I on Lieut Grants horse and gone but a half mile when we heard the report of a cannon very near us and saw a large force of cavalry charging down upon us and the train of wagons that were constantly passing on the pike. They were coming in a direction so that unless we made good time we would be cut off from camp, so without saying a word we put spurs to our horses for camp and my horse, becoming excited I could not hold him flying over the rocks. Where there was more danger of my being dashed to pieces should he stumble than from bullets, but he kept on his feet and I was the first to enter camp, passing Capt Grant and the supposed fastest horse of the regiment. The reg't was already in line and giving my horse to our bugler, I took my place in the ranks. We wished them a happy new year by an effective volley which sent them back in disorder. They mistook us for a wagon train parked as our wagon formed our breastworks on one side and our fire surprised them greatly. They then went at us with their artillery, of which they had two pieces, but doing us little harm as they were poorly managed knocking over all of our wagons and killing some of the horses and mules. One horse they knocked a hoof completely off and it was killed to put it out of its misery. The cavalry went for the wagons passing on the pike, the guards and teamsters taking for the woods and a few coming to camp. Maj Yates conceived the idea of charging on the artillery and was given the right of the reg't to accomplish with the rest remaining inside the works. He ordered us out and Co. A was very well represented, Co H about one half and the orderly serg't was the only one from F, not a man from the other two companies being present. This wild scheme was abandoned as probably every man would have been killed or captured as there could not have been more than 150 men to charge on from 3000 to 5000 well armed and mounted. We went back inside and repelled six charges made upon us. Once they nearly reached our breastworks. They sent in a flag of truce four different times demanding our surrender, unconditional at first when Col Innes made his famous sarcastic reply. (We don't surrender much.) The next time they said they had heavy reinforcements and would slaughter us all if we did not. The Col said he wanted to see their reinforcements first. Next they offered to parole us all and give the officers their side arms, but it was of no avail, though Lt Col Hunton was in favor of it as our ammunition was nearly exhausted. We were finally reinforced by the 10th Ohio Infantry and the 4th Mich Cav, but the fighting was ended. Some amusing incidents occurred. A rebel put spurs to his horse and rode by the pike exposed to the fire of reg't simply to be reckless, but his horse fell dead, pierced by a dozen bullets, though it carried him beyond the range of guns first. It was said his upper lip was shot off. A lot of them with union overcoats on charged up on one side of the camp saying for God's sake don't shoot your friends, but their gray pants told who they were and they were driven back with the loss of their leader whom they sent in to learn if he was dead or a prisoner, but he had fought his last fight. Company D lost one man killed and there were quite a number wounded, some mortally, one Charley Mingo, an Indian in Co. A, died before reaching Nashville. He was shot from the rear and he said it was Col Hunton that did it against whom he had sworn vengeance for punishing him severely for stealing whiskey from the sutler. I saw one man skulking for the cedars and taking good aim I fired when he pitched head long and I congratulated myself for killing at least one reb, but the next day I visited the spot and found no dead man there or any signs of one. We never knew how many of the rebels were killed and wounded, but from some we captured afterwards they said they lost more than in any other engagement they had ever been in before as the cavalry losses were small usually. We lost a great many horses and mules as they were unprotected from the rebel fire. The horse I rode of Lieut Grant's was wounded and had to be killed. At night Capt Grant called for six men to go with him and release some mules that were tangled in the harness and were burning up alive as the rebels had fired the wagons. The night was intensely dark and the expedition a dangerous one as we supposed the rebs were still lurking around. We released several mules that were burning and making piteous noises and coming to an old house we heard talking within and demanding who was there they begged for us not to shoot as they would surrender. It proved to be a lot of our sick and wounded from the front who took us for rebels and we supposed them to be the same. They were overjoyed on learning who we were and went to camp with us. I found two blankets while out and had mine stolen by the 10th Ohio so I was still one ahead. On calling the rolls six of our company were missing, 5 of whom were corporals and the boys called the fight the corporals skedaddle. They struck out for the woods and the account of the tall running they done to keep out of the way of the rebels was amusing. A. D. Welling was captured, taken to Richmond, confined in Libby prison and afterward exchanged and returned to us. I was on guard at night.

Jan. 2.   We strengthened our breastworks, dug a long rifle pit, etc. Drew some rubber blankets which were needed. It rained a part of the night. I was on guard again three hours.

Jan. 3.   It rained most of the day and night, making it very muddy. A courier came in and reported a large force of rebs near us, prepared for an attack upon us. We burned all the buildings and fences and cut down all the trees that would serve as shelter for the enemy. About noon an alarm was sounded and we started for camp. I was nearly half a mile away from a burning house, and being very muddy my wind gave out before I got halfway there. They shouted for me to hurry up or I would be cut off, but I took my time and brought my axe, most of the boys throwing away theirs. The alarm was a false one. The 9th Mich Inf were guarding a train and drew in line to help. At night reinforcements were called for to assist an ammunition train. Co's A & H and two Co's of the 10th Ohio were sent without our supper, expecting an all nights job, but the enemy had been driven off before we reached them with a

Captured at Lavergne on
January 1, 1863, Alva D. Welling
was later exchanged and
returned to his regiment. He
left the army with Kimball in
the fall of 1864 at the expiration
of his three-year enlistment.
(Archives of Michigan,
Lansing)

loss of 10 killed and 15 prisoners we returned to our quarters. I was on guard again three hours at night also the next, making four nights in succesion.

Jan. 4. We were within hearing of all the fighting at Stone River and the booming of the cannon some of the time was fearful and we had orders to stop the men that would get scattered and run for the rear, each of them supposing they were the only survivors of their regiment.[1] News came of the evacuation of Murfreesboro and we were happy again.

Jan. 5. The reg't went out to cut ties. A few shots were fired and the men had a long run to reach camp, but no fight. We had slept out in the

---

1. Kimball is apparently describing the feelings of the men during the several days of battle. Actual fighting near Murfreesboro ended late on the 2nd and the Confederate retreat began late the following night.

mud and rain all the time without tents and I think with me it was the most gloomy week of the war as reports [had] been constantly coming in [of] Rosecrans defeat or a great slaughter of our men.

Jan. 6. Co. H stood picket while the rest of the reg't got out ties. I found two rifles, three cartridge boxes and a knapsack that had been thrown away during the fight.

Jan. 7. We started about 10 o'clock for Smyrna, where we took up our quarters in the houses, Co's A, H, and K occupying the upper story of an old warehouse. A floor was not as comfortable a bed as the ground. Smyrna is a very pretty place, everything looking clean and fresh compared to other towns that have been occupied by troops.

Jan. 8. Co. H stood picket while the other co's built the bridge.

Jan. 9. We had the day to wash and clean up. A report came that the rebel cavalry had captured a train with the Ohio bridge builders. Our wagons were got in a square again. Capt Grant took six of us to search a house for a reb who had been seen but did not find him.

Jan. 10. We started for Murfreesboro through the mud. I was rear guard. Camped near town.

Jan. 11. I was detailed as cook for our squad. Had inspection and dress parade.

Jan. 12. Had a good day for cooking. Darkie John returned, having been driving team instead of being hung as had been reported.

Jan. 13. I baked up about a bushel of biscuit. Drew some fresh beef and fried some.

Jan. 14. Made some beef soup and dumplings. It began to rain about 2 o'clock and rained steady all night. We bought some canned peaches. Charley Fowler and I eat two $1.25 cans. Tent leaked badly but we sang songs and were happy.

Jan. 15. The rain turned to snow and sleet and froze hard. A bad day for a cook.

Jan. 17. Weather more pleasant. Cooked some beans a little too much, they scorched.

Jan. 18. Resigned my culinary duties to W. A. Gavett after cleaning up the kettles. Charley Fowler went to see his brother Henry but found he died the 15th.[2]

Jan. 19. A large detail were sent foraging, I did not go. Cut some wood for Adj't Calkins and carried in his tent for him. Rained at night.

Jan. 20. Was very muddy again. Sutler brought some butter and dried peaches.

Jan. 22. Went foraging in the forenoon, got eight load of corn.

Jan. 23. It was warm and pleasant. Did my washing in the forenoon. In the afternoon had base ball and dress parade at night.

Jan. 25. Dress parade at 4:30 P.M. At night a few collected in our tent and had a sort of prayer meeting. A chapter was read, followed by singing, prayer and speaking; all seemed interested. A similar one was held in Co. F.

Jan 27. The army poet and balladist, as he was called, came to the reg't and sang some patriotic songs. He wished a barrel or box to stand on so he could look down upon our faces. His name was Locke. I bout [bought] 25 cts worth of his songs. He was afterwards discovered by Rosecrans & staff seated behind a rock and on coming near him they saw him secret something under his wig. They scalped him and the paper dropped to the ground, which proved to be a sketch of the fortifications, the number of troop, etc. He was, of course, taken as a spy and I heard executed in due time as such.

Jan. 28. Weather extremely cold with some snow. Drew rations. Had another meeting.

Jan. 29. The whole reg't made preparations for a march to Nashville. Started at 9 A.M. Camped at Lavergne for the night. It was hard marching and Col Hunton marched us without mercy. Had our rations of whiskey at night.

---

2. Henry Fowler served in Company I, Fourth Michigan Cavalry, from August 1862 until his death from disease on January 15, 1863, at Murfreesboro. He was two years older than Charles, having been born in 1840.

Jan. 30. Co's B, C & G remained; the rest of us went on. Co's A & K left on the road. Some of the recruiting officers returned bringing in some recruits. Marched to the Asylum and then countermarched two or three miles, camping on mill creek again.

Jan. 31. The men were set at getting out timber. I had to cut wood for HdQrtrs.

Feb. 1. We drew timber out of the water near the bridge most of the day.

Feb. 2. It was quite cold; worked at the bridge most of the day. The boys confined in Nashville came up looking very filthy. The bugle was blown in three different places.

Feb. 3. It was very cold; worked at the bridge again. I had the flux & quit in the afternoon.

Feb. 4. Charles and I slept in the wagon and did not wake up until after roll call. I got some powders of the Dr., being the first since in front of Corinth.

Feb. 5. I reported sick. It froze hard at night but we slept comfortably in the wagon.

Feb. 6. Felt much better. My principal food was buttermilk at 10 cts a quart.

Feb. 12. Broke camp at 7 and waited for a train until 12 through a rain when we went within a mile or two of Nashville and camped.

Feb. 13. A detail of 13 from each of five Co's were sent on the Tenn & Ala RR, two miles below Brentford [Brentwood], where we built a small bridge and replaced about 20 rods of track that had been torn up, returning at sunset.

Feb. 14. Rained most of the day. Giles Noble worked in my place.

Feb. 15. A squad of 20 of us went to Nashville to church.

Feb. 16. We got out timber for the bridge at Franklin. Had a long scuffle with Bill [Irving?] Thompson, coming out even with him. Rained in the night.

Feb. 19. Co's D, C, & H went to Franklin on the cars but did not work much. Fired at dogs, rabbits, etc., from the train. Very windy at night.

Feb. 20. The same Cos went again. Capt Fox [ordered] no guns to be fired but by some means mine went off at sight of a rabbit when Fox said he would arrest the man that fired the next gun.

Feb. 21. We again went out and have nicely got at work when it began to rain but as the cars had gone back after timber, we had to tough it until they arrived. Reached camp about night.

Feb. 24. Went to the bridge and found the bent down we had raised saturday before. We got up three water bents.

Feb 26. It was storming so we did not go at work. The Brown boys and myself rec'd a box from home with lots of good things in it.

Feb. 28. At 4 P.M. we were mustered for pay; the Col ordering all first class men to be reduced to 2nd that were away without sufficient reason for it.[3]

Mar. 1. I did not attend church in town. Mic Chamberlain was made 8th Corp.

Mar. 2. We found all our bents down and stove in pieces. We got up two again.

Mar. 3. We had 22 men report sick in our company. Got up on the third bent and stringers on.

Mar. 4. A brigade of infantry, a battery and some cavalry started on a four day skirmish from Franklin. Got up the second tier of bents and some stringers on.

Mar. 5. There was heavy cannonading and musketry from the troop who left the day before and we awaited with deep interest the result. Toward night some straggler and the cavalry came and reported a sad defeat, most of the brigade being captured. They were drawn in an ambush by the rebel Van Dorn and overwhelmed by numbers. It was

---

3. The legislation that established volunteer engineer regiments also divided the privates in these organizations into second class or first class, depending on previous experience. Second class received the infantry pay of $13 per month and first class the higher pay of $17 monthly.

expected they would follow and attack Franklin but we met heavy reinforcements when we returned to Nashville.

Mar. 6. We finished the bridge and ran a train over it. It was the best job we ever done. Rained at night and the water rushed through our tent, soaking us well. We always cut a small ditch around the tents.

Mar. 8. A few of us went to the Episcopal Church. Rained at night.

Mar. 9. Was on guard, but being supernumerary stood but one trick Serg't Vandy aided me.

Mar. 11. Serg't Vanderwarker took Chas Fowler & myself as guard, also two others, to search a grocery and house of ill fame for liquors. Serg't V & I did the searching while the others stood guard. The fellow was from Mich and as he treated us well we were not very close in our search, but confiscated a keg of beer. Ordered the shop closed up. The cause was one of the boys got drunk there. Went to Hospital and had our dinners and returned to camp.

Mar. 12. Rec'd three letters. Drilled two hours and had dress parade.

Mar. 13. Had battalion drill in the afternoon. The Col sold two bbls of flour for $1.00 a barrel. Our tent invested their share in postage stamps.

Mar. 15. Went to the Episcopal Church. A part of the reg't received new Enfield Rifles.

Mar. 17. We cleaned up our camp ground, split some shakes and set our tent up higher. Drilled and had dress parade. At night Capt Grant with 8 of us went out to catch some boys around niggers huts but found none.

Mar. 18. We received orders at midnight to march, which we did at 9 A.M. Camped at Lavergne again. The day was quite warm.

Mar. 19. We resumed our march at 8 A.M., passing great numbers of dead horses and mules which smelled terribly. Cross Stone River and camped.

7

Fortress Rosecrans

MARCH 20–JUNE 28, 1863

Murfreesboro was a strategic point for control of Middle Tennessee and had been fought over for more than a year. Rosecrans was determined that it would remain safely in Union hands and serve as a major supply point for further movement southward. Upon completion in late June, the defenses at Murfreesboro were the largest earthen fortification constructed during the entire war. They were eventually designated Fortress Rosecrans in the commander's honor. The Michigan Engineers worked regularly on the fortifications for three months, beginning in mid-March 1863. Most of the outer lines were nearly complete before the arrival of Kimball and his Michigan comrades, but much remained to be done in the construction of inner lines, bombproof magazines, and supply buildings designed to hold 5 million rations.

The construction work was dangerous and several of Kimball's comrades in Company H were injured in accidents. Others took sick and were hospitalized. Kimball notes sadly the sudden death of Henry House and blames the surgeon.

One of the highlights of their stay in Murfreesboro was the arrival of much-needed gear and supplies. Most received new tents and uniforms. Perhaps most important, their twenty-year-old rifled muskets were replaced with the prized Enfield and Springfield rifles.

Kimball also references the arrival of new recruits and an expansion of the regiment with the addition of Company L. Originally structured like an infantry regiment, with ten companies of approximately 100 men, the Michigan Engineers was enlarged following the passage of legislation in 1862 that determined volunteer engineer regiments would have twelve companies with approximately 150 men each. It was not until the fall of 1864 that the regiment reached this authorized size of about 1,800 men. Company L joined the regiment at Murfreesboro, and Company M arrived several months later; the original ten companies grew as recruiting continued through the war.

During their work at Fortress Rosecrans, the men and their officers also were caught up in a growing competition between their regiment and the Pioneer Brigade. The latter unit had been formed by Rosecrans, drawing upon skilled craftsmen and artisans in his army's infantry regiments. The Pioneer Brigade was commanded by Regular Army engineer James St. Clair Morton, who also held a commission as brigadier general in the volunteers. Morton sought in vain to have the Michigan Engineers merged into his command, and he and Innes thought very little of each other. Kimball makes several references to this competition and dispute, both while at Murfreesboro and later during the summer of 1863.

By the middle of June, the work was nearing completion and Rosecrans was preparing his army to move forward against Bragg's Confederates. The main army left Murfreesboro beginning on June 24, and the Michigan Engineers wrapped up their work on Fortress Rosecrans. Before departing, they received several high-level visitors and were inspected by governors Austin Blair of Michigan and Andrew Johnson of Tennessee.

Mar. 20. Worked all day cleaning up our grounds for the camp.

Mar. 21. We were reviewed by Gen Rosecrans and staff at 2 P.M. with our knapsacks and accoutrements on. Marched in common and quick time, which then the Gen addressed us thus. Young men you have worked well. In one instance I know you fought well and you march well. Now do as well in the future as you have in the past and when you return your home state will be proud to place your flag in the State House with your names inscribed thereon. Signed the pay roll. Cos A & C were paid.

Mar. 22. We were paid to Jan. 1st. I rec'd $56.65 besides sutler bill. I bought me a watch for $16.00. Col Innes went home on furlough. We were paid mostly in one and two dollar bills.

Mar. 23. Sent $20.00 home by Capt Fox. Drew seven bell tents. Mic and I got together in No. 4.

Mar. 25. Mic Chamberlain put his watch up for $25.00 in a lottery and his chance in and won it himself. I put mine in at $19.00 and a chance in but it was won by George Green.

Mar. 26. We began getting out timber for a warehouse.

Mar. 29. The wind blew very cold. Wrote three letters, sending $50.00 home this pay day.

Mar. 30. It snowed some. We finished getting timber. Fred McGee cut his foot.

Mar. 31. Our Co went to Murfreesboro and tore down an old warehouse and grist mill for lumber for the warehouse. It was tremendous cold.

Apr. 1. Finished tearing down the mill and killed a lot of rats. Some of the soldiers were selling pies. They would make change by cutting a pie 5cts a quarter.

Apr. 3. It was very windy and cold. Our Co put up rafters. Charley Fowler went to hospital. He sent me his pocket book to keep for him.

Apr. 4. We worked at the rafters again. Gen's Rosecrans, Garfield, & Morton came to see us.

Apr. 5. Was very pleasant. Dress parade at 5 P.M. Sent mother 48.00 as a present.

Apr. 6. Our tent bought a razor. At the end of our service the boys gave it to me as I carried it most of the time. At night heard Col Moody of the 74th [Ohio] preach. He was called the fighting parson. After the war at a reunion he was called to account for saying we gave them Hell, boys, in a charge. He said he was going to say give them Hail Columbia, but the boys only heard the first word and misconstrued.

Apr. 8. Was on guard. Had to stand guard over Low Wing[1] who had been arrested by Lieut Chapel. Set our tents up on shakes, making more room.

1. Lorenzo Wing is the only man in Company H with a name close to this, but available records suggest he didn't enlist until August 1863.

Apr. 9. Our reg't had to go on brigade drill with the Pioneers.

Apr. 10. Again went on brigade drill with the addition of the Chicago Board of Trade Battery and some cavalry. Mustered again for pay.

Apr. 11. Drilled again. There were three batteries on drill. Rained at night.

Apr. 12. Attended preaching at the 74th Oh. Had dress parade. Col. Hunton and Maj Yates inspected the camp.[2] They said Co. H had the neatest and most comfortable quarters of any in the regiment.

Apr. 13. Got out timber for a magazine to store away ammunition.

Apr. 16. A part of the Co put tarpaulins on warehouse for roof. The balance got out timber.

Apr. 17. Was quite warm. Got out timber on the battleground of Stone River. Some of the boys picked up an old shell and uncapping it set a low match to it. The powder flashed with a loud report, driving in into the ground but it did not burst. Many of the men were buried in very shallow graves frequently seeing a hand or foot sticking out.

Apr. 18. Cleaned up our guns and camp and shaded the tents by putting up branches and small trees. Had parade at night.

Apr. 19. Had inspection and dress parade. Heard Col Moody preach again in the evening.

Apr. 20. Finished getting out the timber. Six of us got out three 9 foot sticks during the day.

Apr. 21. Several of us sent home our overcoats by express. I took them to the express office costing us $2.50 each. All soldiers piddling around the depot were arrested.

Apr. 22. Put flooring in the building. Lieut Chapel got on a spree and treated all of us.

Apr. 23. Was detailed to cut wood for the Co. A fellow in Co G died of fever named [William] Reed.

2. Yates was acting as major in the absence of Hopkins on recruiting duty. Hopkins resigned in May and Yates was commissioned in his place.

Apr. 24. Henry House of our tent died at 7 A.M. and was buried at noon. I was one of the escort. He had a tumor in his jaw, which the Dr lanced and it began to swell immediately choking him to death. He the Dr had killed him by trying an experiment. Some of the boys had a disgraceful drunk during the afternoon. Col Innes returned, visiting each Co.

Apr. 25. A lot of us went swimming. I picked some full blown roses.

Apr. 26. Worked at the magazine. Tried Co cooking but had a row and cooked as before.

Apr. 27. Worked at the magazine again. Col Innes turned a cold shoulder to Gen Morton.

Apr. 28. In the afternoon they began filling the magazine with ammunition. During our work on the warehouse and magazine we used water from a little pond near by that was very deep without any apparent inlet or outlet. We afterwards heard that the rebels had thrown several of their dead in it that were afterward fished out. I never believed it but it was not very pleasant to think of. Had several ball alleys and used round shells for the balls.

Apr. 30. Our Co drew a barrel of potatoes. Mustered at 5 P.M. for pay at 6 a man preached to us being a fast day.

May 1. We used poles as flooring for the warehouse. Part of the reg't were paid.

May 2. Co E buried a man named [Arthur] Starke. Had a twin brother in the same company. I rec'd $26.00 for two months. Finished flooring and covering the warehouse.

May 3. We raised $120.00 to send House home, Ezra Stearns to accompany the body but they could net get the papers signed. Had regimental inspection and parade. The Col complimented our Co on their clean guns. A man in Co K died.

May 4. We were sent to get out timber but there was none to be found convenient.

May 5. Cap Grant was carried to a private house in town sick. Were sent to get out timber for another magazine.

May 7. It was cold and rainy so we did not work. The commissary got some white fish.

May 8. Complaints were made that Co H was not getting out their share of the timber so we had extra allowance assigned us.

May 9. Got out our 300 feet of timber quite early. Excitement over Hooker and army.

May 11. It was reported that Richmond was taken.[3] A. J. Walker cut his knee with a broad axe.

May 13. Heard some firing while at work which proved to be target shooting. Killed a snake 5 or 6 feet long which were very scarce. Got out our 300 feet.

May 14. It was very warm and pleasant. Worked as usual. I picked me a mess of greens.

May 15. Was on guard. The night was real chilling.

May 17. I was detailed as cook for our mess. Baked us some dried apple pies for supper.

May 18. I had baked beans for dinner and supper. I weighed 147 lbs without a coat.

May 19. Set rising for bread but did not have good luck. Had boiled pork for dinner.

May 20. I again set rising and had splendid luck. We did our baking in an outdoor dutch oven by filing with wood and heating it and then cleaning out the coals and putting in bread, pies, etc. Capt Grant started for home on a 20 day furlough. I sent a slice of bread home by him.

May 21. Had potatoes for breakfast and a fine bread pudding for dinner.

May 22. Had good luck again with my bread and potato soup for dinner.

---

3. Actually, Hooker's Union Army of the Potomac had been badly defeated in the battle of Chancellorsville.

May 23. Had poor luck with my bread. Went swimming. Maj Hopkins' wife visited our Co, calling at each tent.

May 24. Grosvenor succeeded me as cook. I wrote four letters.

May 25. Began building a magazine in one of the forts.

May 26. Worked again at the magazine. The weather was hot.

May 27. I was on guard in front of head q'rs. We were ordered to shoot after hailing three times. Had to walk our beat all the time and sleep at the guard tent.

May 29. I helped put a cover of brush over the Lieut's tent. It rained some.

May 30. We covered our tents with poles and brush for shade.

May 31. Ingles [William B. Ingalls] hired me to cook in his place for $1.00 for the week. Had reg't inspection and parade. Gen Thomas made Col Innes a visit.

June 1. Made bread and had good luck.

June 2. Had a nice shower in the morning and a heavy thunder shower at night.

June 3. Made some lemon pies and gingersnapps and set rising over night.

June 6. Failed on my bread but baked 26 pies.

June 7. Had Co inspection at 9 A.M. All detailed men were ordered present. There were over 500 men fit for duty and 686 present in the eleven Cos, Co L having joined us a short time previous.

June 8. Had a new recruit named [William] Loomis. Co L rec'd 30 making 71 in their company in all. Counterhewed timber for magazine. Sutler brought some beer.

June 9. Worked again at the timber in an apple orchard. Threw green apples.

June 11. Rained considerably. Some of the boys got wet. I crawled under a stick of timber.

June 12. It was reported a woman and two men were to be hung near Wood's Hd Qrs. About 40 of our co went and stood in the hot sun all day. An immense crowd gathered but there was no one hung. The band made its first appearance playing the tattoo. They did exceedingly well.

June 15. I reported sick and got a dose of Opium, Whiskey, Caster Oil & Turpentine. It cured.

June 16. Had no work so had Co drill. Band played at night.

June 17. Very hot so we drilled two hours after breakfast.

June 18. I was on guard. Quite a number of the boys got drunk and George Waldo got a rail on his back.[4]

June 19. Capt and Lieut Grant arrived. I rec'd Mothers and Amelias photographs.

June 20. Drilled two hours. The 4th Mich Cav band came and played until midnight.

June 21. Had inspection and parade. Our Co mustered 73 men, rank and file present. Co B was the largest & H next. Total officers and men in reg't 742.

June 23. Co's C, G, & H went at shingling a warehouse building built by the pioneers.

June 24. The army made an advance. Heard cannonading about noon. Van Cleves division moved into the fortification.

June 25. It rained all day. Heard more cannonading. At night the 4th Mich Cav band favored us with music.

June 26. We put down platforms for cannon in Lunette Negley. More cannonading.

June 27. We worked on a platform in Lunette Crittenden. Gov Blair of Mich and Johnson of Tenn, afterwards President Johnson, made us

---

4. Meaning Waldo had to carry a wooden rail on this shoulder as punishment for being drunk.

a visit and on parade Blair addressed us, complimenting us, etc. The 4th Cav band played. Capt Grant, to show off, marched Co H by platoons and [the demonstration] fizzled.

June 28. Prof [Henry E.] Whipple of Hillsdale [College] preached to us. Blair stayed overnight in camp.

8

Middle Tennessee

JUNE 29–NOVEMBER 4, 1863

General Rosecrans developed a careful plan of feints and rapid advances designed to drive Bragg's Confederates out of Middle Tennessee. The Tullahoma campaign that followed was a brilliant success, and Bragg's army barely escaped being trapped before reaching the safety of the Tennessee River. Between June 23 and 30, the Union forces suffered fewer than one thousand casualties and cleared Middle Tennessee of enemy forces. The rapid movement and Confederate destruction during their retreat, however, meant that Rosecrans's men found themselves on the north bank of the Tennessee River without the means to force a crossing or resupply. Once again, Rosecrans turned to the Michigan Engineers to resolve both issues.

Innes's command was ordered to repair the railroad between Murfreesboro and the Tennessee River. Kimball was part of a detachment under Lieutenant Colonel Hunton that moved south by rail as far as possible and prepared for the arrival of the regiment. Over the next several days, various companies of the Michigan Engineers repaired railroad and wagon bridges and sections of road that had been washed out by the heavy rains. By July 12 most of the regiment was at the Elk River, where retreating Confederates had destroyed a vital 470-foot-long span. Until it was rebuilt, Rosecrans's army could not be supplied by rail.

The competition between the Michigan Engineers and the Pioneer Brigade again surfaced at the Elk River. Innes promised to do in ten days with only his regiment what Brigadier General Morton said would take several weeks if both commands worked together under his command. Rosecrans took Innes up on the boast and the men worked with a will, completing the bridge in just seven days.

Though Elk River remained the regiment's headquarters and base for operations for several months, the companies of Michigan Engineers worked on a wide variety of construction and repair projects. Some built the pontoon boats and bridges that Rosecrans used to take his army across the broad Tennessee and on into northern Georgia. Others, including Kimball and Company H, got out railroad ties and worked to repair some of the railroad branch lines.

The summer of 1863 also marked the first time that the Michigan Engineers worked alongside black soldiers. Former slaves were organized into companies and whole regiments at Elk River and several other places across Tennessee. Some of the regiment's noncommissioned officers were detailed to serve as drill instructors, and several work expeditions were organized with both white and black companies, such as that described by Kimball on July 31. It's not clear what Kimball thought about this development. He generally calls the black soldiers "darkies" or "niggers," yet he comments on their work alongside white troops without the kind of negative or condescending disparagements often found in the writing of Union soldiers. Most likely, after two years of war, he was perfectly willing to share the danger and work with anyone willing to serve. The black soldiers whom Kimball served alongside eventually became members of the Twelfth and Thirteenth regiments of the United States Colored Troops (USCT).

Rosecrans's army was badly defeated when Bragg's army pounced on it along the banks of Chickamauga Creek and drove it back to Chattanooga by September 21. Confederates took possession of the high ground that dominated the supply line as it approached Chattanooga, and the Union army was on the verge of starvation or surrender. Federal military authorities rushed reinforcements from both Virginia and Mississippi, but it would take time for these to arrive, and Wheeler's Confederate cavalry was sent to disrupt the long supply line leading from Nashville to Chattanooga.

For most of October, companies of Michigan Engineers labored along this route to save the Union Army of the Cumberland in Chattanooga. Two companies constructed the pontoon bridge that opened an alternative supply route at Brown's Ferry downriver from Chattanooga, while others constructed storage buildings at Bridgeport to hold all the supplies being forwarded to that point for use by the garrison at Chattanooga and the growing relief force. The balance, including Kimball and Company H, worked under Innes to repair the damage done to the Nashville and Chattanooga railroad line by Wheeler's raiding Confederate cavalry. By early November, their efforts and those of thousands of others had restored a reliable supply line to Chattanooga, and reinforcements were being forwarded with the goal of driving Bragg's army back into Georgia.

In addition to the deep, probing raids by Confederate cavalry, the summer and fall of 1863 saw the emergence of an even more bitter war behind the lines. Not only had official Union policy become increasingly harsh on civilians aiding the enemy, policy wavered between protecting loyal civilians and prosecuting a hard war; sometimes the difference was hard to measure. Kimball and his comrades were in the thick of it.

It was a time of frequent alarms, and the Michigan Engineers' expeditions into the country were more frequently probing for guerillas than for provisions. Though most escaped the random attacks, Frank Foster of Company A was killed by guerillas in October, several from Company E were taken prisoner south of Elk River, and Franklin Hogle of the same company was captured while part of a foraging party. Kimball was part of the unsuccessful search party. The hardest-felt loss, however, was that of Captain James W. Sligh of Company F, who was fatally injured in a train wreck caused by Rebel-sabotaged track. The increased organization and aggressiveness of Confederate guerillas made the countryside an increasingly dangerous place for Union soldiers like Kimball and his comrades in the army's rear area.

June 29. About 400 rebel prisoners came in Murfreesboro. We were ordered to march at 10 A.M. Ten from each Co were to go with Col Hunton on the RR. I was one of the number. Went as far as Christiana then took the pike and camped with the reg't. Had a shower, the reg't getting wet but we did not. Whiskey at night.

June 30. We took the RR again and reached Wartrace at 3 P.M. the roads being bad the reg't failed to come so Col Hunton told us to make ourselves as comfortable as possible. Mic, Dode [Alva D. Welling] & myself eat supper at a darkies and then went to a white mans who let us sleep in a good feather bed, it being the first time I had done such a thing in the confederacy. He also gave us a good breakfast. We found 2 1/2 miles of track torn up between Fosterville & Bellbuckle.

July 1. The reg't came up about 10 A.M., rested awhile, and went in camp. Some of our cavalry came up and taking us for Rebels drew sabers and were about to charge when they found out their mistake. Some buildings burned at night. Had plenty of fresh pork. We captured two prisoners.

July 2. We marched to Duck River Bridge and went to work. Weather very hot. I was on picket.

July 3. Eight of the Co's, including ours, went two miles farther where some trestle had been cut down and began repairing that. At night Capt Grant wanted me to carry a dispatch on horseback to Wartrace but as I was sent by railroad instead of going with the reg't, I didn't know the way, and Mic went in my place. Several rebels came and gave themselves up. We had three hogs for our mess.

July 4. Finished the trestle in the forenoon. During the afternoon a shower came up and Capt Crittendens son, who was telegraph operator for us carelessly rested his arm on his instrument and was struck by lightening. He was carried out in the rain and in pulling off his socks the skin came off with them, but he recovered.[1] Dr. De Camp tied his horse near a hive of bees which it upset and the bees charged on horses, mules, and men. The mules and horses broke loose and stampeded over the hills lively. The Dr's horse was stung to death. It was amusing to see the mules dance and caper. Our men brought in five conscripts from the rebel army.

July 5. Lay in camp all day. Made out new muster rolls. Nothing to eat but pork and hard tack and for supper no pork but coffee.

July 7. Meat once a day. 35 guns were fired over the capture of Vicksburg. Chewed up our ground which had been an old rebel camp and stink bad enough.

---

1. Jason Newton Crittenton was a young civilian telegraph operator in the employ of the Union army. He survived his injuries and later joined the Michigan Engineers as a commissioned officer in 1864.

July 8. Ten from our company and two trains went out after ax handle timber but found a two year old beef and two hogs instead.

July 9. We put a wall to our tent from an old secesh tent. The band came out for the first time on parade. Some of the boys got up a show.

July 10. Six of the cos went with Col Hunton to Elk River to build a bridge.

July 11. The rest of us marched at 5 A.M. for Elk River. Went at work in the afternoon. Johnny Green gave up his team of mules and I took them. There had been a large cotton mill destroyed by fire here and one of the finest water powers for its size I ever saw.

July 12. Rosecrans & Staff came to see us. The Col told him we could build the bridge in 10 days. Morton of the Pioneers wanted 30 days with his whole brigade.

July 13. The men went at work at the bridge. A bent fell injuring Serg't [*illegible*]. I did not work my team.

July 14. The horse teams drew timber in the forenoon and mule teams in the afternoon. We drew rations of sugar and potatoes.

July 15. Finished drawing timber in the forenoon. Gen Palmer & Reynolds passed by our camp. Had a swim but the water was cold, mostly spring water.

July 16. I did not work my team. Got most of the upper bents up. About 60 prisoners passed by.

July 17. I hauled tools and ax handle timber in the forenoon. Finished the upper bents and got some stringers on. Mic was not allowed to sleep with me in my wagon because he did not get up for roll call.

July 18. Weather hot. Bridge complete by 4 P.M. and a train run over, the band playing Hail Columbia. Col Innes went with the train to Decherd where he telegraphed Rosey [Rosecrans] of the completion of the bridge and rec'd a very complimentary reply. For a large job it was the best and quickest done of any we ever undertook.

July 19. Lieut Grant rec'd his resignation papers. Several trains passed the bridge.

Elk River Bridge Built Under Col. Innes Personal Supervision in Eight Days. Officers in foreground Surgeon Wm. H. De Camp, Captain J. W. Sligh and Adjutant C. W. Calkins.

Constructed in July 1863, the Elk River Bridge was one of the most important repair projects that Kimball and the Michigan Engineers completed. Retreating Confederates had destroyed it, and Union troops lacked a secure railroad supply line from Nashville until it could be rebuilt. This image was taken as the Michigan Engineers labored on the bridge. (Sligh, *Michigan Engineers*)

July 20. We fixed up a fine plan for swimming. Some darkie troops camped near us were out drilling.

July 21. Lieut Grant started for home. Had blackberry pie for supper.

July 22. I went early with six other teams to Decherd for rations. I had three bbls sugar and three sacks coffee. The head of one bbl came out and I stocked up.

July 25. I went to Decherd again after rations. Bought 6 bbls flour, 2 bbls peas, 1 rice, 1 salt, and a cask of hams for officers use. We rec'd pay. I rec'd $46.00.

July 26. I sent $20.00 home. Had inspection, some rec'd a [*illegible*] for dirty guns.

July 27. The reg't went at getting out timber for a bridge down the road. [*Illegible*] split his big toe completely in two with a broad axe.

July 28. Some of the boys from the different co's got up a show. Gave the teamsters free tickets for the use of their wagon covers to make a tent of and charged 50 cts admission. Of course it was crowded and they took in $115.00. It was a very creditable affair. The reg't got out ties and we hauled them.

July 29. Sutler got on some goods, beer with the rest and Co F indulging too freely, some of them got in a fight.

July 31. Co's G & H with a company of darkies went to widow creek to put up a bridge. It was all framed.

Aug. 1. Went to Decherd after corn but could get none.

Aug. 2. I picked a mess of greens and got some green corn.

Aug. 3. I gave my team to Grosvenor. [William] McKenzie, wagon master, did not like it and wanted the Capt should have me return it.

Aug. 4. Asa Hudson & I picked some huckleberries & blackberries and buying some milk had a feast. Had parade at night.

Aug. 5. A detail from Co H went as train guard to Tantalon.

Aug. 7. Some of the boys caught an eel which was cooked, and a good many got a taste of it. It was the first I ever tasted. Co A was sent to Mud Creek, Ala, to put up a bridge.

Aug. 8. Our co had 100 ties to get out or 4 to a man. A part of us finished before noon and some failed to get out their number when Capt Grant sent all back without our dinner to get out the required number.

Aug. 9. I was detailed as cook. Had inspection by Col Hunton and Adjt Miller.

Aug. 10. Drew for rations hard tack bacon coffee & sugar. It was poor grub.

Aug. 12. Col Innes was made superintendent of the N & C RR.

Aug. 14. I got some one to cook for me and went as train guard over the mountain to within 7 miles of Stevenson. Had a heavy shower. We did not start back until 11 P.M., reaching camp at three the next morning.

Aug. 20. About 500 more darkies came. I had four to draw ties with or load ties.

Aug. 21. The reg't were getting out timber. I was on guard. We had a box in the ground and when any of us from our tent were on guard at the quartermasters tent we would be sure to find something in the box next morning. A ham and some loaf sugar was in it this time. Such rations were for officers but we got a share.

Aug. 27. We were ordered to get out ties. A citizen came in with peaches to sell but did not realize much for them, the boys were stealing most of them.

Aug. 28. Cos A, D, G, & L went to Stevenson and B to Murfreesboro.

Aug. 29. I was on guard was very chilly. Joe Lake got asleep at his post.

Sept. 1. We had five ties each to get out. Just at night Capt Grant called for 15 men to go with him after some rebels who were reported near. We found no rebels so we went on, searched two houses and had high times. We found a revolver in one of the houses and I got me a nice blanket. Reached camp at 4 A.M. I had a splendid horse to ride.

Sept. 2. We were excused from work all day. Some of the boys were lame and sore.

Sept. 9. We were in line of battle at 3 A.M. as rebels were reported near.

Sept. 10. I was on picket. Some rebs fired on a nigger picket post and they kept up a firing all night. In the morning traces of blood was found and also where they tied their horses. The reg't lay on their arms in line all night.

Sept. 11. At 10 at night ten men were called for to get a train on the runoff near Duck Creek. Found 9 cars off, worked all night and finished about noon, then went to Wartrace to let some trains pass us and reached camp about midnight of the 12th.

Sept. 21. We put us up a splendid little fireplace in our tent. Weather quite frosty, especially the nights.

Sept. 23. We were called out in line of battle at 3 A.M., remained until daylight.

Sept. 24. There were four from each co sent to Tullahoma for rations. A train arriving reported 3000 rebels in Decherd. Had to remain until near night. The camp had quite a scare in consequence of it. It proved to be but a few guerillas; their Col. was captured.

Sept. 25. Five Cos of the 102nd Ohio came to reinforce us, also some darkies. We were out in line in the morning as usual.

Sept. 27. Had a very rigid inspection and but six guns in the Co bore inspection, mine being one of the number. The rest were sent to their quarters to scour up. There was some tall swearing about it.

Sept. 28. Got out timber for another bridge in case this should be destroyed.

Sept. 30. Finished framing three bents which was the portion assigned to our Co. Several trains loaded with troops passed to the front. Gen Howard in command.

Oct. 1. More troops passed to the front. Gave my gun a thorough cleaning.

Oct. 3. A part of the 3rd [Twelfth] Corps, Gen Slocum commanding, passed by.

Oct. 4. Mic and I ran the guard and got some sweet potatoes and chestnuts. Saw a rebel cavalry horse hitched in front of a house but not having our guns we let him stay there. The rebs captured McMinnville and we began to fortify. Worked until 11 P.M.

Oct. 5. Went at foraging again. Were in line of battle at 3 A.M. The 2nd Mass & 13th NY of the 12th Army Corps reinforced us.

Oct. 6. We were sent foraging for our reg't & the 2nd Ky battery. Twelve of us in Co H were mounted. We killed 36 sheep out of a flock of 40, also a hog or two. They were thrown in the wagon and we returned to camp all sound. Rec'd orders to march at a moments notice.

Oct. 7. I was sent with the teams to Garrison Fork where Wheeler had destroyed the bridge. The Cos came by rail bringing timber with them.

Oct. 8. Went at clearing away and framing. Had a company of darkies to help us. Worked until after midnight finishing all but laying the track. It was 210 ft long, 25 ft high. Pretty good days work.

Oct. 10. Returned to Elk River again. I went with the wagons.

Oct. 13. Very rainy and tents leak badly. I went out to the cook fire and found John Griffith of the 107th NY, an old York State acquaintance, trying to buy some bread as they were short of rations. We did not recognize each other at first. He ate a hearty supper with me and we had a good visit.

Oct. 14. Went over to visit John and found them just starting for Estelle Springs. Found a number of old acquaintances with him.

Oct. 19. Started as team guard but only went as far as the station. Frank Foster of Co A was shot and killed by the guerillas.

Oct. 21. Fred Smith of Co B while crossing the bridge missed his footing and fell 53 feet. The Dr said he could not live but he did.

Oct. 22. We rec'd our mail, the first for a week.

Oct. 23. A brigade of the 12th Corps passed to the front, the 107th NY being among them. It was the last I saw of John as he was killed at Atlanta. Col [John B.] Anderson succeeded Col Innes as Supt of the RR. Some guerillas tore up the track four miles from camp and ran off a train. Capt Sligh was on board and had both legs crushed from the effects of which he died. Our train was just behind and the boys made sad havoc among some sutler goods on board.

Oct. 24. I was on guard at the commissary tent. We had a ham for breakfast as a result. Very cold but had a fire to stand by.

Oct. 25. A man in Co E went out in the country and stayed a week. He was sentenced to carry a rail four hours a day for forty days and to be on fatigue duty the balance of the time.

Oct. 27. Co H was sent to a house to watch for rebs. We laid in wait until 2 o'clock when a dozen of us were sent to another house to search that but as usual found nothing. Reached camp at 4 A.M. Air chilly.

Oct. 29. Had Co drill in the forenoon and had formed for battalion drill when Col Hunton ordered the roll called in Co M and about half of the men were missing. He then dismissed us.

Oct. 31. We were mustered for pay. Col Hunton acting as inspecting and mustering officer. I was promoted to 1st class at $17.00 per month, having received but $13.00 per month since I bolted and was reduced.

Nov. 1. One of Co M men was buried, the band officiating for the first time. I was cook again.

Nov. 2. Our teams went after forage and Hogul [Franklin Hogle] being told by a citizen where he could get some turkeys, left the train and that was the last we ever see of him. The boys got some potatoes, beets, pumpkins, etc.

Nov. 4. Capt Grant took 20 of Co H and went in search of Hogul. Found where the rebs had stopped his mule and captured him. It was afterwards reported he took the rebel oath of allegiance and joined their army as they allowed him to choose between that and being hung.[2] Pete Gordon threw Joe Fairchild clean through our tent from the inside in a scuffle. It took them the rest of the day to mend it.

2. Accounts of Hogle's disappearance conflict. No further record has been found.

9

The Nashville
and Northwestern

NOVEMBER 9, 1863–MARCH 12, 1864

By this time a large Union army was gathering near, or was en route to, Chattanooga, and with it came a growing demand for food, ammunition, livestock, and the other tools of war. Even if the Rebel forces were driven back from Chattanooga, a reliable and secure rail line was necessary, and Nashville was the most important point from which supplies could be forwarded. Nashville itself, however, like the line further south that Kimball and the other Michigan Engineers had labored to repair in the previous months, was also vulnerable to Confederate mounted raids and guerillas.

A single railroad line from Louisville to Nashville provided one route for supplies, but it had been cut several times during the war by Confederate cavalry and remained vulnerable at many points. Though Nashville was located on the broad Cumberland River, it was not a reliable water route for large supply steamers during periods of lower water. Clearly, another supply line was needed. Union authorities turned their attention west from Nashville to a partially completed line that linked that city with the Tennessee River near Waverly, Tennessee.

Dubbed the Nashville and Northwestern Railroad, this line had been started before the war. A February 1863 study conducted by Major Yates of the Michigan Engineers laid out the remaining work. About eight miles of track were in place running east from the Tennessee and about twenty-six running west from Nashville. The intervening gap was about forty-four miles long and some of it was partially graded. The hilly route would require several long bridges, not to span large rivers but rather to ease the grade. In addition, the railroad crossed the Harpeth River seven times in a ten-mile span. Completion required a force of bridge builders and railroad men supported by a large force of laborers. The Michigan Engineers were to provide the first two and black infantry regiments the latter, with Colonel Innes in overall charge of the line's construction.

Since the line's route included few populated points, the working locations were generally referred to by their distance from Nashville. Section 49, where Kimball worked for a time, was between forty-nine and fifty miles from the city. Kimball worked in this area through late November as part of a detachment guarding a survey party.

At various times, as many as four or five companies of the Michigan Engineers were working on the Nashville and Northwestern, beginning in September 1863. Kimball's Company H arrived on November 10 and remained on this duty until March 1864, when the Michigan working parties were near section 55. Since the First Missouri Engineers and Mechanics were responsible for the railroad beyond that point, the Michigan men were pulled from this railroad and given new orders.

Though the territory around the Nashville and Northwestern was less vulnerable to roving Confederates than the Nashville and Chattanooga, there was still risk as Kimball and the others in Company H worked and foraged in the neighboring countryside. The Union command provided a small defensive force to guard the Michigan Engineers and USCT regiments, and Kimball frequently comments on this bitter war involving the Eighth Iowa Cavalry and other units against Confederate guerillas and mounted units.

Despite the risk, however, Kimball and his comrades were regularly in the countryside, foraging to supplement their meager rations. As he noted in his journal for November 24, "such expeditions were the spice of life with us." He also noted that day the presence of a pro-Union man named Adams who guided the party. Tennessee remained a bitterly divided state, and the area behind the lines was filled with both those intent on killing Union troops and those willing to risk their lives to aid them.

Kimball and his comrades also worked alongside many of the same black soldiers they had known back at Elk River in the summer of 1863. These were the men of the Twelfth and Thirteenth USCT regiments, former slaves commanded by newly commissioned white officers. Among the company-grade officers were men promoted from the ranks of the Michigan Engineers.

During this time, the company continued to receive recruits as regimental authorities sought to fill the unit up to its authorized strength of eighteen hundred men. These men's arrival was the result of President Lincoln's call in October for another three hundred thousand recruits to serve three years. If states failed to meet their quotas, they must resort to a draft in each community coming up short. A federal bounty of $300 each was offered to encourage enlistment, and local communities sweetened the pot by as much as $200 more in order to avoid the stigma of a draft. The Michigan Engineers gained about eight hundred men during just a few weeks of recruiting, with at least seventy assigned to Company H. Kimball frequently notes the arrival of parties of recruits as well as their vulnerability to camp diseases and amateur accidents.

In addition to filling the ranks of enlisted men, the regiment also sought to bring its officer corps up to full strength. Legislation allowed each volunteer engineer company to have one captain, two first lieutenants, and one second lieutenant. Captain Marcus Grant remained in command of the company, but the vacancy of his kinsman Solon Grant had not been filled since he resigned in July 1863. In addition, Second Lieutenant Harry Chapel had been absent sick for much of the summer and fall of 1863.

Effective January 1, 1864, the company's new command structure was formalized. Captain Marcus Grant would continue to command, and Lieutenant Chapel moved up to the senior first lieutenant position. The other first lieutenancy went to former first sergeant Albert Vanderwarker. The second lieutenancy was given to Orasmus (or Osmer) Eaton, a fifty-four-year-old businessman and officeholder from Allegan County with no previous military experience. Kimball and his comrades were angry to see outsiders arriving with commissions, and Eaton was put in the difficult position of proving himself after his arrival in early February. Since Kimball's many references beyond the first one lack any negative comments, perhaps Eaton was successful before he left the service in October 1864.

Harry J. Chapel, another original member of Company H, was eventually promoted through the ranks to the position of first lieutenant. His surname was misspelled in this printed image. (Sligh, *Michigan Engineers*)

The proximity of Nashville while Kimball was traveling to and from the railroad line afforded him the chance to take in some cultured entertainment. En route to the new assignment, he took in the Tchaikovsky opera *Mazeppa*, which featured actress Kate Fisher, a well-known leading lady of the day. Several months later, while returning to Nashville from building the railroad, Kimball attended performances of Tom Taylor's melodramatic plays *The Ticket-of-Leave Man* and *Still Waters Run Deep*. These were both making an American tour after successful launches in London, though Taylor is better known to history for his production *Our American Cousin*, which President Lincoln was enjoying the night he was assassinated at Ford's Theater.

Nov. 9. Pitched tents. I visited Will Gavett at the hospital and took dinner. Attended theatre at night, Play Mazeppa by Kate Fisher. Froze some.

Nov. 10. Went by rail on the Nashville & Northwestern RR to Co A, 32 miles from Nashville.

Nov. 13. Eight from each Co were sent out foraging. Our mess fared well as we got five sheep, some sweet potatoes, pumpkins, etc.

Nov. 17. Dan Bennett & myself were sent to the station after tools. At night an alarm was given and the darkies reforming in camp. We thought the rebs were upon us for sure, but it was a false alarm.

Nov. 18. Several of the boys got tight and came near having a row.

Nov. 19. Shumway, Hotchkins, & Kinch were arrested for being drunk. Capt Grant gave me the Col's revolver to carry to him which was loaded, but the Col wanted me to fire it off and clean it. I went back in the woods, set up a mark and fired at it when Capt Hannings came up very angry and wanted to know by whose authority I was shooting at that time of day. I told him by the Col's. He doubted my word and demanded my name and Co when he made inquiries of Capt Grant about it and was informed that I knew my business. The Col was well pleased with the cleaning.

Nov. 22. Our Co was to get out 400 ties but only 268 could be counted. Hotchkins and Kinch were reduced to $13.00 per month.

Nov. 23. We went six miles further and camped. Stormed some.

Nov. 24. Twelve men were called for from Co H to accompany Maj Yates, Lieut White, and Charley Ball, a government spy, to Sec 49 to do some surveying for the railroad. I was one of the number detailed, but not feeling well some of the boys wanted to go in my place but as such expeditions were the spice of life with us, I was determined to go although I had a presentment that I had better remain. We were all mounted and started at noon. Found the 13 U.S. Colored encamped there, the pickets taking us for rebels were about to fire on us when we made known to them who we were. We here found an old man named Adams who had nine sons all union men who had lain in the woods for a week in fear of being murdered by guerillas if they stayed at home. One of them told us they would take us where thirty guerillas stayed the night before and thought they would be there then. the Maj being pretty full of whiskey proposed we should go and capture them, so with

Adams for a guide we set out, seventeen in number, all told, to make the capture. We were following a bridle path in single file when a noise was heard and a halt ordered. Very soon we heard a hoot owl lift up his voice near us but thinking it might be some signal from the enemy we proceeded cautiously. As for myself, I had read the Indians considered it an ill omen to hear an owl so near and I wished myself home, but we followed on and came to a valley where we dismounted and one half held the horses while the rest were to charge on the house and shoot—bayonet and capture all within. the Maj assigned Walker and myself to go to the back door with bayonets fixed ready to stop any that tried to get away while he and two or three others were to enter at the front door and demand a surrender, the rest being in readiness to support. They entered the door and found three or four old ladies almost frightened to death but no men. We returned to our horses, mounted, and started down the road at full speed, scattering out for some distance, when a few of us in advance saw an object running from a house and two or three shots were fired at it, but it got into the woods when the Maj rode up excited and said we were shooting at our friends. It proved to be one of the Adams boys who had ventured home that night and had gone to bed when his wife heard us coming and supposing we were rebels, told him and he made for the woods with nothing but his shirt on his back. His brother, by a signal, called him back and explained the mistake, he riding behind with the Maj did not think his brother was home. We then returned to camp and struck out in another direction two or three miles to an old guerillas house but found him away though his family were yet up. We had orders to search the house and found a crock of butter, poultry, etc., which we considered contraband and took with us to camp where we arrived late in the night and slept in an old house where the darkies had a picket post. We had just got asleep when one of the pickets fired and we up and out to inquire the cause. The darky said he saw some men down in the woods nearby. We rushed down in the woods and as I was going by the pickets I heard one remark Dems brave me see dem go. We found nothing and the Maj accused the picket of being scared and firing at nothing, which he denied. The Maj told them if they shot again and hit no one he would shoot them so we went to bed and had a good sleep.

Nov. 25. Capt Grant took four of us with Adams for a guide to an old distillery after whiskey and returning we scoured the woods for rebels

John B. Yates was the original commander of Company A; he replaced Enos Hopkins as major and then William P. Innes as the regimental commander. Yates was the major architect of the work along the Nashville and Northwestern during the time Kimball and his comrades were laboring on it. (Sligh, *Michigan Engineers*)

but found none. The nigger pickets leveled their guns at us again, but we made them understand who we were. The Maj with the rest of the men done the surveying and we reached camp at night. We invited the Maj to eat breakfast with us also the other officers telling them our friend had sent us a box from home. A darkie had dressed and cooked the fowls with butter and all enjoyed it hugely. Altogether it was one of the most pleasant times we had during the war.

Nov. 26. We were payed four months pay. I rec'd $63.70. We sent the money to Nashville to buy us some stoves. During our absence [Ross] Swift had cut his hand with an axe and was sent to Nashville where he soon died.[1]

Nov. 28. It rained in the forenoon and several of us went over to the nigger sutlers and were having a gay time when word came the Co had gone at work. We still remained until we spied Lieut Chapel coming when we rattled out of that lively and went at work.

Nov. 30. Our band and Pete Gordon left for Nashville. Pete received a lieutenancy in a colored regiment.

1. Swift's injuries became infected and he died in a Nashville hospital on January 6.

Dec. 1. My birthday being 21 and weighing 153 lbs. Wrote several letters.

Dec. 5. The teams went to the station after supplies. When near our old camp the boys found some letters written by us that had been opened and robbed. I had one with $10.00 in it for home that went all right and one with $5.65 in it for the albums that was taken.

Dec. 7. The camp of the 8th Cav was attacked and two men wounded.

Dec. 15. Cos A & H marched to sec 49 and encamped. Got some straw, etc. Heard cannonading supposed to be gunboats on the Tenn River.

Dec. 16. Cos I & G came up, it was rainy and cold. We helped them pitch their tents and get settled.

Dec. 17. We climbed a tree for a fox squirrel. I cooked it for us.

Dec. 20. Ten men from Cos A, F, & H went with Maj Yates to sec 53 to survey a new route where there would be less grading. I assisted in carrying the chain and we were gone all day. The rest did not work.

Dec. 22. Worked in the woods. A man in the 8th Ia Cav shot himself while cleaning his revolver. Some said it was intentional.

Dec. 23. Co H went foraging on Yellow Creek ten miles distant. I captured a goose and some cabbage. The boys of our tent got fresh pork and turkeys. One of the boys chased a hen in the house and captured her while the old lady looked on in horror.

Dec. 24. We got out square timber. The 8th Cav captured 12 rebs and brought them in camp.

Dec. 25. It being Christmas we did not work. Some of the messes had roast turkey. We had stewed chickens and sweet cake.

Dec. 29. We were [assigned] 100 feet of timber to a squad. We got through at noon.

Jan. 1. This was known in Mich as the cold New Years and snow fell two inches with us so we did not work.

Jan. 2. We went out at work. I frosted one finger. There was 22 axes broken by frost.

Jan. 3. We had a turkey stuffed and baked in each tent of our camp. We lived well while building this railroad.

Jan. 5. The wagon train came with rations and mail. Killed two horses coming up it was so icy. A mule fell on Aaron Decker and broke his leg.

Jan. 7. Orders rec'd for four roll calls a day on account of the men leaving camp without permission. Got out timber and ties as usual.

Jan. 11. Cut wood and prepared a coal pit for burning.

Jan. 13. Cos A & H put bents together for a trestle. Co F went foraging but did not return.

Jan. 14. Five of us went with Lieut White to get a draft of the trestle.

Jan. 17. It rained all day. A lot of new recruits came. Roberts boys [cousins Latham and Isaac Roberts] and Lyman Jones.

Jan. 20. More recruits making 47 for Co H up to this time. I rec'd some socks and mittens from home.

Eighteen-year-old John Thibos was one of almost nine hundred recruits, about whom Kimball frequently commented, who joined the regiment in the winter of 1863–64. (Archives of Michigan, Lansing)

Jan. 24. Twenty of us from Co. H were sent to the station for guns, rations, etc.

Jan. 25. We started back going twelve miles. About 25 more recruits came up with us.

Jan. 27. Finished the trestle which was quite a long one.

Jan. 29. One of our recruits named [John A.] Potter died. He said he enlisted to save his son from coming and he thought he would soon get his discharge as he was 40 and in poor health. He got it sooner than he expected. All of us had ten ties each to get out. I finished mine in the forenoon.

Feb. 1. Four of us were detailed to get up Co wood. More recruits came and some of the recruiting officers. Two recruits came as lieutenants, one of them Osmer Eaton for Co. H, and many of the old soldiers were justly indignant.

Feb. 2. Went to the R.R. trestle two miles from camp to get out timber.

Feb. 6. Finished raising the bents at the trestle.

Feb. 7. Three of us in our mess planned to have some fresh pork as one of the boys had discovered some hogs in the woods a short distance from camp. We had to manage so as to avoid detection and arrest. Charley Hoyer was to shoot it and myself and another were to butcher it as soon as shot and drag it safely away from camp and dress it while Hoyer was to hide his gun and act as a spy to throw the Serg't of the guard off our track. It worked successfully and he brought a wheelbarrow and placing the pork on the wheelbarrow covering it with a coffee sack and piling stove wood on top we secured some fresh pork. A few minutes after the hog was shot another shot was heard. It proved to be two recruits from our Co on guard named Lewis Ritter and Chas Spaulding practicing bayonet exercise with loaded guns when the hammer of Ritters gun caught in his belt and discharged hitting Spaulding in the right breast and passing through him and over the camp. It served to detract attention from us as the Serg't of the guard, upon hearing their shot, left our track and started for them. Spaulding was carried to camp where he died during the day, 3 P.M. He was a sailor and married, being the second husband his wife had lost in the war.

He commenced to tattoo the Goddess of Liberty in the arm of one of the boys and it was half finished, leaving a lasting memento for him of Spaulding.

Feb. 8. Got out our ten ties in the forenoon and buried Spaulding in the afternoon. I was one of the escort and a Universalist preacher in Co. A said a few remarks.

Feb. 9. I was on picket. There was a dance at night and some of our boys went.

Feb. 16. It was quite cold. Co's F & G moved to sec. 55.

Feb. 17. Co's A & H moved to sec. 55 and secured a good camping ground. Very cold at night.

Feb. 18. Got out timber in the forenoon and built me a bunk in the afternoon.

Feb. 19. I helped to get out timber in the forenoon and draw in the afternoon.

Feb. 20. I had charge of hauling the timber for Co's A & H. Co. F did the loading and unloading.

Feb. 21. Had inspection at 9 A.M.

Feb. 25. In getting out timber I cut my foot and returned to camp.

Feb. 26. Foot quite sore. Remained in camp and wrote letters. The boys sent to the Tenn River for RR iron returned.

Feb. 29. It rained all night and froze as fast as it came.

Mar. 1. We were awakened by the limbs of trees loaded with ice breaking and falling. One crashed through our tent but injured none of us. Some in other tents were hurt more or less. Cut all the trees in camp.

Mar. 3. Sent all the sick to Nashville in preparation for marching.

Mar. 5. Started at 1 P.M. on our march for the station. Camped within four miles of Charlotte. Had the ground for a bed and it was cold.

Mar. 6. Marched to the station. My foot was quite sore but I kept up. Some of the recruits were about used up.

Mar. 7. It looked very stormy. I was detailed to go after hay. Had a good time. Col Dorr of the 8th Ia cavalry was reported shot by guerillas near Waverly.

Mar. 8. Co's F & G went to Nashville. I was on guard over some East Tenn refugees in the forenoon and on picket at night.

Mar. 9. Co's A & H came through to Nashville and camped near the small pox hospital. Rained all night.

Mar. 10. Got a pass and went up town and had a negative taken. Attended theatre at night. The play was The ticket of leave man.

Mar. 11. Attended theatre again. Play: Still the water runs deep.

Mar. 12. Mic was absent at roll call and was arrested but released again. Rec'd my photograph.

10

Railroad Blockhouses

March 13–June 27, 1864

The Nashville and Northwestern could help ensure that supplies reached the forward base at Nashville, but the long railroad route further south was still very vulnerable to roving bands of guerillas and raids by Confederate cavalry units. Sabotaged railroad track could be quickly replaced but the key bridges and storehouses couldn't. It was obvious that Union forces would be moving south from Chattanooga toward the Rebel base at Atlanta, which would only increase the reliance on a single railroad track for supply and reinforcement over a longer route. The answer was to protect all key points along the long railroad route leading back to Nashville.

In addition, Union railroad officials determined they could accelerate the delivery of supplies south if they repaired and defended the Nashville and Decatur (also known as the Tennessee and Alabama) line. This route ran southwest from Nashville to a junction with the Memphis and Charleston road at Decatur on the Tennessee River. With this route in operation, railroad officials could operate a one-way triangle, with loaded trains running from Nashville to Bridgeport to be unloaded and then back to their base along the Memphis and Charleston and Nashville and Decatur. Even if this scheme wasn't always utilized, the Nashville and Decatur line would provide a secondary route for supplies and reinforcements being shipped south. Of course, this also meant there were more railroad lines to be maintained and defended.

Union commanders had experimented with different types of railroad defenses up to this point, with mixed results. The key was to design a structure that could house a small garrison and stand up to an assault by dismounted cavalry. It was expected that raiding enemy cavalry might have light artillery but not heavier field pieces, and would be reluctant to remain in an area for long. During the spring of 1864, Lieutenant Colonel Hunton of the Michigan Engineers was involved in a series of experiments using different styles and thicknesses of wooden defenses and various artillery pieces and small-arms fire. The design result was a square blockhouse structure, built from the standing timber found in abundance throughout the region.

Though actual defenses varied with the needs and resources at each crossing, a typical blockhouse had two stories. The lower was often constructed of a double thickness of wood laid horizontally, with a second level containing a single thickness of wood, often set at an angle to the lower to allow full defensive fire in all directions. In other cases, the lower level was covered by banked earth, with a single level showing to the attackers. In either case, the roof was comprised of timber to protect against plunging artillery fire. Usually the initial and more complicated construction work was done by men in the Michigan Engineers and then garrison troops finished by moving dirt and removing trees that the enemy could use for cover to attack.

Beginning in March, eight of the twelve companies of the Michigan Engineers were pulled from their various assignments, such as the Nashville and Northwestern Railroad, and shifted over to building these blockhouses along the railroad. Kimball and his comrades in Company H were sent to work on the line running from Nashville to Decatur as part of a four-company battalion under Major Yates that also included Companies A, F, and G. The companies were divided into squads and spread out along the route, with each squad assigned a specific blockhouse. Kimball was part of a squad assigned to build a blockhouse about five miles from Columbia, Tennessee. It was probably the one protecting a crossing of the Duck River or one of several at the many Rutherford Creek crossings.

After completion of their assigned work, Kimball's squad and the others were moved further south along the railroad to build blockhouses closer to the Alabama state line. Kimball was also detailed to work at the company headquarters. By the middle of May, he was working on a

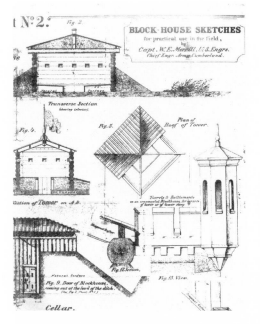

Blockhouse designs were prepared by army engineers following tests of various styles, conducted in part by officers of Kimball's regiment. Kimball worked on the construction of several in 1864. (Buell-Brien Papers, Tennessee State Library and Archives)

This blockhouse is nearing completion, and the image demonstrates its strategic role in defending railroad bridges such as this one over Running Water in the Whiteside Valley. (Francis Miller, *Photographic History of the Civil War*)

blockhouse at Mud Creek, north of Athens, Alabama. Once work was done there, Kimball's squad was moved east along the Memphis and Charleston to Crow Creek near Stevenson. The bridge there was about 265 feet long and required the defenses provided by a blockhouse.

During this period, Kimball noted the return of many men who had been detailed on various duties. This was part of efforts to eliminate the practice of relying on field regiments to staff rear-area responsibilities, such as hospital steward, and strengthen the fighting units in advance of the expected spring offensive into northern Georgia.

Supply lines secured, thanks in no small part to the Michigan Engineers, Major General William T. Sherman moved his army of sixty thousand further into northern Georgia in May 1864 as part of a concerted Union effort to press the Confederacy on all fronts. Sherman's objective was Atlanta and the important Confederate industrial and railroad facilities located there. His advance south from near Chattanooga involved a series of flanking attacks through rugged countryside, always remaining in contact with his critical supply line astride the Western and Atlantic Railroad. By the middle of May, he was pushing beyond Resaca, and he then continued on past Calhoun, Adairsville, and Kingston. By the middle of June, Sherman's forces were across the Etowah River and closing in on several heights north of Marietta. Meanwhile, Kimball and his comrades continued work to secure the long supply line.

Mar. 13. Struck tents at 7 A.M. and loaded everything on the cars. Each Co. was divided in 5 squads, a non-commissioned officer in charge of each. A lot of tools and 17 days rations for each squad. Went on the Tenn & Ala R.R. to put up stockades at the bridges and trestles. Corp Updike with our squad stopped within 5 miles of Columbia. Had plenty of straw to sleep on.

Mar. 14. Ground up our tools and built an oven out of the old castings from a burned bridge. There were 23 in our squad and we did no guard duty.

Mar. 15. We commenced getting out timber 12 x 18 for sills, posts & plates and 12 x 12 for covering over the roof. The posts were set on end, making an 18 inch wall with portholes and dirt to be out on the top to make them bomb proof. We bought some potatoes and butter and contracted for milk for our coffee. It is a fine farming country one of the best in the South and very wealthy.

Mar. 16. Signed the muster roll for pay. [Albert] Roberts cut his leg. Very cold and snowed some. Froze hard at night.

Mar. 17. Some warmer. Tapped some maple trees. [Lyman] Jones cut his wrist with a hatchet.

Mar. 18. Lieut Chapel drew our pay and brought it to us. I recd $31.00.

Mar. 19. Rec'd the first mail of the week. I had two letters.

Mar. 20. I took a stroll in the country and bought some eggs. Some of the boys got a hog and a sheep.

Mar. 22. One of the track hands was robbed of $55.00 by a guerilla named Bailey.

Mar. 27. [*Illegible*] and myself went in the country and bought [*illegible*] dozen eggs. We called at the residence of Brig. Gen Voorhees, C.S.A.[1] His mother, an old lady, was at the house. We obtained the best food from the surrounding country at this camp of any while in service.

Mar. 28. One of Co. A men was taken prisoner by guerillas. He made his escape, but had his fingers shot off by the colored soldier at our camp accidentally fired his gun, slightly wounding him.

Mar. 29. Very cold. We commenced framing.

Mar. 30. Capt Grant came down and gave us a blowing up for not pushing the work more, saying we were behind all the rest but we were doing the best job of any. He ordered all the sick out for work.

Apr. 1. It stormed so did no work.

Apr. 2. Finished framing sills and plates and commenced at the posts.

Apr. 3. It was Easter and eight of us had five doz eggs. Six of us went out to explore a cave some distance from camp. It was so suffocating

---

1. Colonel William M. Voorhies Sr. of the Forty-eighth Tennessee commanded a brigade at various times but never received the promotion to brigadier general.

two of the boys had to back out. It is said the cave was known only to a colored man previous to the war. His wife was sold to a southern planter and he hid her in the cave supplying her with food. She gave birth to a child while there and it became totally blind in the darkness of the cave. It seemed wild to everything but its mother when brought to the light. The negro was to be taken south with the rebel army when knowing she would starve he revealed his hiding place. Lieut Chapel came down and ordered us all out to work. He sent Jim Pope after us with orders for us to return to work. He found us with orders for us to go back with him. He reported he could not find the rest. I went to the Widow Voorhees and had a very pleasant visit with her granddaughter Miss Robina Voorhees, a fine looking and accomplished lady of 13. The old lady thought I might be a relative of some of her ancestors were named Kimble and I said nothing to discourage her in her belief. She had two husbands and by the first, named Nicholson, she had a son AOP Nicholson who was U.S. Senator from Tenn at the commencement of the rebellion. Just two years ago today we were on our way to Pittsburg Landing.

Apr. 4. It was a very rainy day but we had to work. Laid the foundations for the blockhouse.

Apr. 5. Finished getting out the timber. Our colored troops had orders to march but they were countermanded.

Apr. 6. Put up nearly one side of the blockhouse, the darkies assisting us. Called on a man named Alley in the evening and had a good visit. He was a spy for Gen Slocum.

Apr. 7. Quite warm. Our colored soldiers started for Nashville. The 8th Tenn Cav came to guard us in place of the darkies.

Apr. 9. Put up the ends. Capt Grant said it must be completed in one week. There was about 2400 cubic feet of timber in it, all taken from the stump. Dimensions 53 x 21 feet on the outside.

Apr. 10. Several of the boys from other squads came to see us. Spent the evening at Voorhees. During the night the cavalry fired two shots and we hustled out [of our tents] but it proved to be some loose horses crossing the creek. Some of the boys were considerably alarmed, fearing an attack.

Apr. 13. A part of Chamberlains squad came to help us put on the plates. Greased some T rails or railroad iron and skidded them up.

Apr. 14. Drew rations. At night just before bedtime the cavalry fired at and chased three men out of camp who were sneaking up to the guard. The cavalry fired about 20 shots but hit no one. The firing was heard at headquarters of the Co and they stopped the trains which ran back to Columbia and reported Forest fighting us. About 5000 troops were started out to help us. Some cavalry came to learn the cause.

Apr. 16. We tried to put on some of the covering but failed for want of help. Some more Tenn Cav came and relieved those guarding us.

Apr. 18. Received help and got the covering all on.

Apr. 23. A few of us remained to finish the job. The rest went to help build the stockade north of us. Moved tents and baggage. Ed Osband came up after an absence in hospital of about two years.

Apr. 24. Too cold for comfort.

Apr. 25. I rec'd a package of albums costing me $11.30 and sold them to the boys, getting $20.00 for them. Commenced getting out timber for the bridge.

Apr. 26. David Johnson came up after an absence of over two years. He had been detailed as secret police in Louisville. He was a very intelligent man.

Apr. 27. Did but a little work. Fred McGee cut his foot.

Apr. 28. Finished getting out the timber. Maj. Yates inspected the stockades and pronounced the one we built the best of any and that Co H was doing the best work of any company.

Apr. 29. Had a heavy shower at night and our tent leaked so badly some of the boys were driven out of bed. George Gavett came. He had been hospital Steward at Nashville for a long time and was an excellent nurse.

May 1. I was out in the country all day. Got some eggs.

May 3. I washed my own and Cap Laphams blankets in the forenoon. They got perfectly dry. Finished putting up the posts.

May 5. To warm for comfort. Hank Kinch and [John] Kalts were sent to Bridgeport sick.[2]

May 6. I started for work but Lieut Eaton ordered me to head quarters to help Charley Fowler make out pay and muster rolls. We did but little at them and went to Gregorys at night where we met six young ladies, all rebels and all loaded with arguments for their cause. Had a very good supper.

May 7. We worked at the rolls in the afternoon and carried Lieut Chapels things to Duck River station as Squads No 1 & 5 were expected to go ahead. We went to the Widow Greens at night. She was a very pleasant woman and intelligent.

May 8. Had orders to finish the rolls, which we did by working all day. Lt Chapels squad passed by.

May 9. Signed the payrolls and an order for Capt Grant to draw our pay.

May 10. Had a terrible storm at night, blowing down our tents, soaking beds, blankets, men, and everything.

May 11. Quite cold. Capt Grant started for Huntsville with the pay rolls but returned.

May 12. I returned to camp, it having been moved to Smiths Station. Our squad killed six hogs but gave Mic three of them. A car was left for us to load our stuff on.

May 13. We loaded on our things and left at 9:30 A.M. Chamberlains squad was left at Pigeon Roost near Pulaski. We reached Huntsville about dark and left at 9 P.M. for Mud Creek, arriving about 2 A.M. Slept without tent as it was so late.

May 14. We split shakes to set our tents upon making more roomy and built bunks so we were very comfortable. Lt Eaton stops with us and eats.

2. Kalts, or Kalls, died at Bridgeport on July 26.

May 15. We built an oven, ground up our tools, and got ready for business. Lt Eaton went to Stevenson and bought himself a set of tin dishes and some tea.

May 16. Commenced work getting out timber and worked hard. Dimensions of Stockade 21 x 21 outside.

May 18. Finished getting out the timber. Between one and two at night we heard firing and the trains coming from Huntsville suddenly stop. The long roll beat in the camp of the 56th Ill and we also turned out. One Co was sent up and soon after myself and four other of our squad started on out own hook. There was such a dense fog we could scarcely see. We heard considerable fighting as we were going along. The infantry had deployed out and had not got there yet when we arrived. We found the train a complete wreck except the engine and two cars that passed safely over where the track had been torn up. The rebels had torn up some track and then going up the track a short distance waited for the train and fired into it. They knew the engineer would open the throttle if they did not shoot him and make a more complete wreck but the speed carried the engine safely over. The engineer was a brother of Gen Custer and was wounded in the hand. A brakeman was nearly killed. As I came up to the train I heard a man talking about someone being crazy, meaning the injured brakeman, but I did not know it and passed along when a fellow jumped out from behind the wreck at me and I thought it was the crazy man sure that had grabbed me, but he grasped my hand and said Hort. I was never so glad to meet a friend in my life. It was Daniel Bennett of our Co who was one of the mail carriers for the regiment. We remained until daylight and returned to camp. The rebs left when they heard the infantry coming.

May 24. Showery all day and a hailstorm in the P.M.

May 25. Quite warm. We placed the sills in place. A lot of bridge builders came to put up a truss bridge.

May 26. Finished counter hewing the posts. Updike went to Paint Rock and Lt Eaton to Bridgeport.

May 28. Finished framing. Borrowed some blocks of the bridge builders and rigged up a gin pole. Lt Eaton sent [John S.] Gordon and myself to Stevenson with $10.00 to invest in sutler goods as he didnt take much to army chuck. We got a barrel of potatoes of the Sanitary committee[3] free of charge and bought some sutler goods. Slept at the Sanitary. A reg't of 100 day Ind troops came in.

May 29. We got our potatoes on the train and rode back. I found four months pay for me at camp, $68.00.

May 30. Had a detail from the 56th Ill to help raise the posts.

May 31. Got ready to put on the covering. Drew rations and for meat we got ½ bacon and codfish.

June 1. The 56 Ill were relieved and the 11 Ind Cav took their places. Got on the plates.

June 5. Very muddy. Had just gone to bed when a dispatch came to move to R.R. as the 2 o'clock train would stop for us. Train on time. Loaded on and went to Crow Creek 3/4 mile out of Stevenson. Got but little sleep during the night.

June 6. Put up tents and then went to Stevenson. I expressed $80.00 home, making $400.00 sent home since enlistment. Some of the boys got quite happy.

June 7. Fitted up our tools. Squads 1 & 2 with Co HdQrs went to Bridgeport.

June 8. Began getting out timber. Put a foot bridge across the creek to get to the spring. Had a heavy shower.

June 9. Our meat gave out and we bought some ham and sourkrout.

June 10. Updike started for Bridgeport for clothing. Owls and mosquitoes very thick. The owls would come in camp at night and hoot and fight. We suffered but little from mosquitoes the camp fires driving them away.

June 20. Drew ten days rations. Got a barrel of cider vinegar, which was quite a rarity as it was mostly made of acid.

---

3. The Sanitary Commission was an extensive volunteer civilian organization that provided food and other necessary supplies as a supplement to army rations. The group had representatives in the field with all major Union commands.

June 22. Two teams came to haul timber. Gordon and I loaded it. Went to Stevenson at night. Quite a number of wounded came in from the front.

June 23. Ezra Stearns cut his knee badly with an adz. Dan Bennett promoted to corporal. The Co took a vote. Stearns, Bennett & myself were the candidates. Stearns rec'd a majority but the Capt interposed and promoted Dan. Fred McGee was reduced.

June 25. Very hot. I rec'd four letters. Lt Eaton went to Nashville.

June 26. Went after some blackberries. Traveled around five miles and got half a pint.

June 27. Mic Chamberlain was sent to us and [Albert] Roberts ordered to the Co. Our meat gave out.

11

---◆---

Supplying Sherman's Army

JUNE 28–SEPTEMBER 24, 1864

By early July 1864, Sherman's forces had pushed the Confederate army across the Chattahoochee River to within a few miles of the outskirts of Atlanta. As his army advanced, however, Sherman's supply line grew longer and more vulnerable while his opponent's shortened. It was critical for the Union forces to repair, defend, and maintain the single span of railroad track stretching back through northern Georgia to Chattanooga. In August, Confederate cavalry under General Joseph Wheeler struck the critical railroad once again.

Detachments of the Michigan Engineers were all along the route, scattered in small details working on blockhouses and other defenses. Kimball and the detachment from Company H at Stevenson had moved to the regimental headquarters at Cartersville, Georgia, by this time. They were among those threatened as Wheeler's Confederate cavalry moved northward with four thousand troopers against the railroad line in George and Tennessee. Though Cartersville was not attacked directly, the men remained on alert as Confederates struck nearby positions. Other Michigan Engineer detachments were not as lucky, and several members of the regiment were killed, wounded, or captured by the Confederate cavalry during this raid.

For the rest of August and most of September, Kimball and the men in Company H remained at Cartersville, working on several local projects. At one point Kimball and his friend Charles Fowler were detailed to clean up the company records, which entailed coming up with some

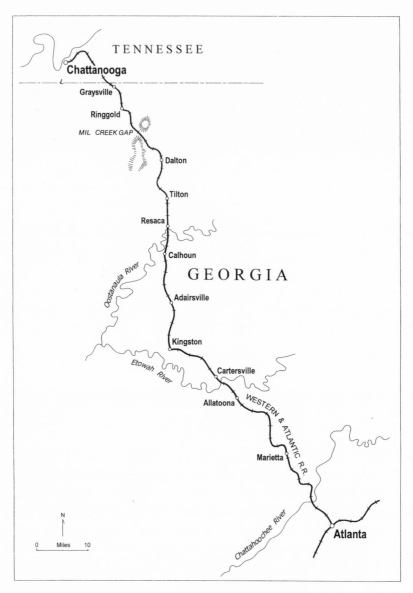

Chattanooga to Atlanta. (Map by Sherman Hollander)

creative explanations for missing arms, clothing, and tools. This was part of the growing army bureaucracy and consistent with the fact that the three-year enlistments of the original men would soon be expiring, including Kimball's.

June 28. The Co. went to Ga. We finished framing posts.

June 29. By a little shrewdness and lying we managed to draw five days rations.

July 4. Worked awhile in the morning and then went to Stevenson. There was speaking but we were too late to hear it. Cannon were fired. We returned to camp and had a blackberry shortcake and bread pudding then fixed up a spring board and had a good swim.

July 5. Lt Eaton returned. Finished the stockade in the forenoon and a car came for us in the afternoon. We loaded up and went to Stevenson and stayed over night, getting our suppers at the soldier's home.

July 6. Left Stevenson at daylight and reached Chattanooga at 10 A.M. Remained there the rest of the day. Mic and I went out and found Lt Pete Gordon. Lt Eaton quite roiled to think we could not get our car billed and go on.

July 7. There was an accident on the road so we could not leave. A sutler got some of the boys to put three trunks containing goods on our car. He got us a pail of beer when he was arrested, his trunks thrown out and confiscated. He said they were very valuable. We confiscated some small coffee pots he had.

July 8. We left at 9 A.M. and went as far as Kingston and stopped for the night. There was about 100 guerillas intending to attack our train, but our cavalry got after them and captured 40 of them, chasing the rest away.

July 9. Went on to Cartersville where the regimental Hdqrs, Co I and a part of Co H were. Put up bunks and got nicely settled down.

July 10. We were to have had inspection but Capt Grant and Lt Vandy were away and did not return until night. I was detailed to assist burying a mule.

July 11. We built an oven and cook shanty. Drilled some, the recruits drilling by themselves.

July 12. I was on guard for the first time in over four months.

July 13. Went out two miles after blackberries and got a fine lot of them. Was an escort to the grave of a man named [James] Wallace, Co. A. The band accompanied. James Davis died just at night.

July 15. Lieut. Eaton an old Californian, Charley Fowler and myself went out in search of gold without success.[1] Lt. Eaton thought the looks of the country indicated gold. We were at the creek one mile north where some of our Co were building a stockade when a splash was heard and going to the creek we saw a horse swimming out and a cavalrymans hat floating away. He was riding by when it is supposed his horse reared and fell upon him in the water. Dan Beckwith dove several times before he brought him up. George Gavett did all that could be done to restore life, so a Surgeon said who soon came, but it was of no avail. He belonged to the 10th Ohio.

July 16. Went with the teams after hay. Had to mow it. A man from Co. F. was buried.

July 20. Had a dance. Joe Fairchild got pretty [drunk]. I was about two hours getting him to camp.

July 21. Help to fit up a store for a man named Benham. The stores had been torn to pieces for firewood by the soldiers.

July 23. Gen McPhersons[2] remains passed by and Gen Grierson who was wounded.

July 26. Helped Chapels squad to put the covering on their stockade.

July 29. Gen Joe Hooker and staff pass on the cars. Also Gen [Judson] Kilpatrick.

---

1. Eaton was one of several in the regiment who had been to the California gold fields before the war.
2. Major General James B. McPherson, commander of the Union Army of the Tennessee, was killed in action on July 22, 1864, in fighting near Atlanta.

Aug. 1. Was sent to the depot after clothing before breakfast. Then helped to dig a grave for one Co G man. Was one of the escort over his remains. At night was guard over Paymaster Rhodes safe.

Aug. 2. The officers had a dance but had too much whiskey they broke up at 10 oclock. Gen. Kilpatrick was there and his boots was the biggest part of him.

Aug. 3. Went out foraging in the forenoon and helped make out muster rolls in the afternoon. Co worked cutting wood. Got a fresh porker.

Aug. 8. [Edmund A.] Austin was buried. Co H had a dance at night. I bought a number [of chances] and danced twice but there were too many outsiders to be pleasant. The rebs cut the road at Dalton so no trains passed. At night a band serenaded Gen [Edward M.] McCook but a few rods from us. Some of us went over to hear the music. Col Hunton saw us and sent a guard to arrest us. I eluded the guards and escaped.

Aug. 16. Lewis M. Rich died and was buried. Considerable excitement as several thousand rebs are reported near here. The return of Benj K Harris who deserted at Perryville and was captured in Northern Mich cutting and with his revolver on the log near him. He was sentenced to be shot, but it was commuted to hard labor on the Dry Tortugas without compensation.

Aug. 19. We were in line of battle at 3 A.M. and remained so until daylight. Trains running. Col Innes thought there was not wood enough being cut and wanted every man accounted for. Co. H showed up 24 men on special detail, as many more on regular detail, and about the same on the sick list. Charley Fowler and myself were on regular detail to right up the Co records and papers. We found them in bad shape and had to charge up the clothing, arm, & tools that could not be accounted for to those that had died and the Capt. would testify that it was correct. We had to go back to the commencement of our service as a Co. Capt Grant had been notified by the War department that unless he accounted for everything his pay would be withheld and he could not get an honorable discharge.

Aug. 20. Our mail and rations came. The latter were much needed as they ran out the 15th.

Aug. 31. 103 new recruits came for reg't. 13 for Co. H. We began making out the muster rolls.

Sept. 1. Finished the muster rolls and began on the pay rolls. Drew rations.

Sept. 4. Lt Vanderwarker went off with the new recruits to place them in their respective companies. Sam Fletcher of Co A had been accused of striking a guard and had been punished for sixteen days in succession by being tied up by the thumbs and standing on the head of a barrel. Today the Dr had him taken off the barrel, saying he had been sunstruck and would not have lived five minutes longer on the barrel. It was said he swore vengeance on the officer ordering so severe a punishment.

Sept. 10. [William H.] Vanortwick was buried. Charley and I have had nothing to do for a week for want of blanks, and Wheeler is reported between Nashville and Chattanooga.

Sept. 11. A large mail and plenty of blanks come.

Sept. 12. Albert Roberts caught Sam Bailey asleep on guard and arrested him. He was sent to the Provost Marshall in town to await court martial.

Sept. 13. Over one hundred more new recruits came.

Sept. 14. More recruits came about midnight. [George E.] Tibbits was caught trying to steal a shirt from a recruit. He was tied up by the thumbs for two hours. Stood on a barrel two hours and had to go without his supper. Gen Smiths band came at night and serenaded our Col. They then went to another place to play and our band went over to serenade Gen McCook and playing the same piece the other band had just played, started a rivalry between them and they played alternately until 2 o'clock when our band got to full of McCooks whiskey to play longer and quit. I was a candlestick for our band.

Sept. 15. I found Japp [Jasper] Godfrey among the recruits and had a good visit with him. Bill Courtney, Low Wing, Ben Taylor & Cott [Carlton?] Noble reported sick but the Dr would not excuse them and they were arrested, a rail strapped on each of them and made to carry it four hours.

Sept. 16. Capt Grant and Lieut Eaton came back from Nashville where they had attended the Court Martial of Mollie Reynolds.[3]

Sept. 18. We were busy all day issuing clothing.

Sept. 23. Co's A, B, C, F, G, & K joined us. More recruits.

Sept. 24. The Co drilled. Had regimental parade etc. Sam Bailey was released without sentence.

3. It is unclear who this is.

12

Discharge and Home

SEPTEMBER 25–NOVEMBER 17, 1864

Sherman's forces took Atlanta in early September after hard fighting. His chief engineer, Captain Orlando M. Poe, issued orders for the scattered companies of Michigan Engineers to report to Atlanta. Several companies reached the regimental headquarters at Cartersville on September 23. Two days later, they continued the march southward, this time with Kimball and his comrades in Company H as part of the column. They crossed over the Chattahoochee River on September 26. In the morning, all but Company H continued on to Atlanta while Kimball and his comrades were left at the crossing. They remained there for several weeks.

Confederate general John B. Hood's army wasn't powerful enough to drive Sherman out of Atlanta, but he decided to move his forces around to the west and then up toward the Tennessee River, hoping to draw Union forces out of the city. Sherman followed for a while, but then returned to Atlanta and prepared for future operations. Details of the Michigan Engineers repaired some of the railroad damage done by Hood's forces. Most of Company H remained at the Chattahoochee River crossing, though details were sent to various points.

The three-year terms of the original 1861 Michigan Engineers were coming to an end, including that of William Horton Kimball. These men had been given a chance to reenlist for the duration of the war early in 1864, including the offer of a thirty-day furlough home and bounty payment, but the majority refused. Because so many experienced men were about to leave the regiment, some were offered an officer's commission if they changed their minds. Kimball was among them but didn't budge. After three years in the ranks, he was focused on going home. On October 27, Kimball and most of Company H marched to Atlanta to join the other nine companies already there. Companies L and M remained stationed in Tennessee.

After Kimball's comrades in Company H reached Atlanta, there were almost 500 original members of the regiment gathered together for the first time in more than a year. Of this total about 375 were going home while the balance remained as reenlisted veterans or officers. Of the Company H men with whom Kimball had first trained back at Camp Owen in the fall of 1861, there were still 62 with the regiment in October 1864, and 56 of them were leaving. In addition to these, however, Kimball was also saying good-bye to many of the recruits who had joined since 1861, including close friend Edd Lapham. As he noted in his journal, "Some tears were shed at parting."

Kimball and his comrades remained in Atlanta while the formalities were being worked out. Kimball and a few others were assigned to help fill out the mountains of paperwork that accompanied so many men being mustered out. The rest of the regiment continued to work on destroying military facilities and nearby railroad track as Sherman was preparing to leave Atlanta on his famous march to Savannah. The general was determined to leave nothing beyond that could aid the Rebel cause once his army left.

The departing men were officially mustered out of federal service on October 31 and received a pay installment on November 1. The next day they drew weapons for personal defense while traveling home since Rebel guerillas continued to attack Union troop trains. Their time with the army was drawing to a close.

As large bodies of men were mustered out of the service, they remained together in military formations when moving from the front to their home states. Kimball and his comrades traveled from Atlanta to Michigan escorted by officers who had also joined in 1861 and decided to resign their commissions and go home with the original men. Among them were Colonel Innes and Lieutenant Colonel Hunton.

On November 3, Kimball and the rest of the departing men were formed up and marched to the railroad station, escorted by the regimental band. They loaded on two trains and headed for home. It was a long journey, and their route took them by so many familiar places: Cartersville, Bridgeport, across the bridge at Elk River, past Murfreesboro, and into Nashville. The journey was not without incident and discomfort but still, they were heading home.

Leaving Nashville, they rode the familiar route on the Louisville and Nashville that they had labored so many times to repair, then crossed the Ohio River by boat. They loaded back up again and finished their journey by rail through Indianapolis and Toledo, arriving in Detroit on November 13. After several delays, they were finally paid off on November 17, and Kimball took the train to Jackson and then the final few miles to Sandstone. He was finally home.

On that same date, most of the rest of the men remaining in the Michigan Engineers were east of Atlanta, on the third day of their march with Sherman from Atlanta to the sea. Their route could be marked by the devastation they left behind and the harsh fate dealt out to Union foragers caught by Confederates, a reflection of how hardened attitudes had become between the occupiers and occupied.

Sept. 25. Broke camp and marched at 7 A.M. A part of Co H were the advance guard and balance in the rear. Went in camp at Big Shanty, marching about 18 miles. The rebs burned a train between Ackworth and Big Shanty. Some of our men claimed to have seen some of the rebs watching us but no demonstration was made against us. The country was stripped of everything and very desolate.

Sept. 26. Resumed our march, a part of Co H being the advance guard, the balance at head of reg't. I was with the advance both days. Passed Kenesaw Mountain and numerous breastworks. Passed through Marietta, which was a beautiful place. Went through to the Chattahoochie river and camped on the South bank. It was a hard march, many of the men giving out. My feet became sore but got there in good shape otherwise.

Sept. 27. Had a foot race between Cap Lapham and a Co G man for $4.00. Co G beat. Dress parade.

Sept. 28. All of our battalion except Co H marched at 7 A.M. for Atlanta. We had orders to move within the works after the others left. Had a nice camp ground and good water. Quite rainy.

Sept. 29. We ditched tents. Policed the grounds and got in good shape. Gen Thomas passed to the rear on the train.

Sept. 30. I was one of 16 detailed to go with teams to Atlanta for rations. It was nearly night before we got them and two wagons remained for forage. I got excused and found the 102nd [107th] N.Y. and learned of John Griffths death. He was cooking a kettle of beans and had them set on some bomb shells and he supposed the powder had been removed. One of them exploded from the effects of which he died in a few days.[1] Saw some others of my acquaintance. While gone my gun was lost or stolen. Two teams left for camp about sundown and going out on different roads missed each other. There were 8 guards and but four guns. The worst shower I ever saw came up and opened on us when about half way to camp. It was terrible dark and the lightening was fearful. The harness broke and altogether it was very unpleasant. We were liable to be attacked at any time by guerillas. Doc Walker came to me and said when he had been in a dangerous place, I always happened to be along and we had come out all right. He proposed that we should walk near each other and if we were fired upon, we would stay together and if necessary take to the woods together as the other guards were no good. Doc was a good natured courageous fellow whose mouth was large enough for a bootjack and the tobacco juice was always oozing from the corners and proficient in swearing but a good soldier. We reached camp about 10 that night, drenched to the skin, hungry and tired. The other team was behind us and came in soon after we did.

Oct. 1. The other men and teams came with forage and three head of cattle for beef. A brigade of infantry came from Atlanta saying it was expected the bridge would be attacked. [Brigadier General Robert] Mintys brigade of cavalry also camped near. Went after muscadines and found a vine. They were similar to grapes but grow singly instead of clusters on the vine. Rained at night.

1. Military records for John J. Griffith, Company H, 107th New York, state he was wounded in action on May 25, 1864, and died of wounds in Chattanooga hospital on August 21, 1864.

Oct. 2. Both of the wagon bridges and one span of the R.R. bridge were washed away before morning. We canvassed our Co as to their choice for president. Lincoln received 98 votes and McClellan 23. Some who had always been democrats said he war had cured them of democracy. Another span of the R.R. bridge washed away. A pontoon bridge was put across. More troops came. A recruit named [Aaron] Wing was a preacher and wanted the boys should listen to his sermon. He had quite an audience until the cooks sang out that dinner was ready and he was left alone in the middle of his sermon. It cured him of preaching in the army. We heard heavy cannonading down the river. It is reported Braggs [Hood's] whole army were crossing to get to our rear, which proved true. Two more pontoon bridges were put across.

Oct. 3. Troops and teams were crossing all day going after the rebs in the rear.

Oct. 4. Troops and teams still crossing. Saw Maj Gen O. O. Howard, commanding Army of the Tenn, Gen Jeff C. Davis, commanding 14th Army Corps and the man who shot Gen Nelson in Louisville. Also Brig Gen Rausow [Rousseau]. Got orders to make out the muster out rolls for our Co. just at night. Charley and I set up until midnight to finish them.

Oct. 5. The troops and teams finished crossing at 1 P.M. One of the Pontoon bridges was taken up. Co. H was kept busy keeping the flood wood away from the bridges. I went to Atlanta on the train at night to look for my gun. Stayed with 107th N.Y.

Oct. 6. Could not find my gun but got another in place of it. George Green was there and we could not get a pass to come on the train so started on foot and took the R.R. track for it. It was nearly night when we started. Capt Grant sent by us for a canteen of whiskey. We walked fast and became thirsty. Drank from the canteen and refilled it with water again. Reached camp just at dark and was never better pleased to get back in my life. We told the Capt a few days after our diluting the contents of the canteen. He said he thought it was damned thin whiskey when he drank it.

Oct. 7. Cos C, F, & G went to Marietta to repair the R.R. destroyed by Hoods army. Fortifying strongly at this point, fearing an attack.

Oct. 8. Very cold all day with frost at night. Issued clothing to the co.

Oct. 9. The Co went to Marietta to guard our wagon train through. Very cold. My gun was found in Co G and Dode [Welling] brought it to me. I had put a red glass set in the stock so it was easily identified. I saw it at the close of the war in Jackson, Mich. when the reg't came to be mustered out. One of the boys bought it of the government and carried it home. The R.R. bridge here was finished.

Oct. 11. One of Col Smiths orderlies named Gregg was shot by rebels a mile and a half from here while carrying dispatches to Atlanta. He was nearly dead when found and died before reaching camp.

Oct. 13. We had drawn three beeves [cows] for 10 days rations of meat. One was killed and the other two we were trying to pen up when one got ugly and charged Dan Morehouse, bucking him in a deep R.R. cut, injuring him considerably. Both beeves got away and it was a wonder for they were so poor they could scarcely stand. We would kill the poorest for fear it would die of starvation. Some singers were out serenading but got to full and happy to do it well.

Oct. 15. We rec'd our mail. I had four letters. Drew some beef and five days rations.

Oct. 17. Capt Grant came from Atlanta in a Majors uniform having been commissioned as such.

Oct. 18. About 350 head of horses and mules were captured by the rebs about two miles from here. They had been driven out to graze.

Oct. 19. A large forage train went out from here. A train of cars was captured by the rebs near Vining Station and burned. We saw the smoke very plain.

Oct. 20. Another train was fired into between here and Atlanta. The engineer broke the train into [two sections] and [one part] reached Atlanta. The other part came back to the bridge as it was down grade all the way.

Oct. 21. Our forage train returned well loaded.

Oct. 22. To cold for comfort. Most of the men built fire places in their tents. All in our tent were old boys and having but a few more days to stay thought it would not pay us. Two trains loaded with rebel prisoners went north.

Oct. 23. Cos C, F, & G went back to Atlanta. Marched all the way from Alatoona.

Oct. 24. Maj Grant came from Atlanta with muster out rolls, discharge blanks, etc. He also offered Charley Fowler and myself commissions if we wished to remain with the regiment. I had no desire to stay, but Charley was inclined to do so but did not. Some of the boys urged me to accept and remain with them. Dell Parsell who had been detailed in the harness shop to repair the harnesses came back to the Co to act as orderly Sergeant when we went home.

Oct. 25. Very busy all day making out papers. Edd Lapham went to the reg't as Qr Master Sergt. The old men were relieved from duty at night.

Oct. 26. Lt Chapel got angry because the old men would not turn out for roll call. Turned over to the proper officers our guns and accoutrements. Had to pay for everything that was missing. I turned over all but canteen, haversack and castle.

Oct. 27. We went to Atlanta at 1 P.M. Some tears were shed at parting with our old comrades. Cap [Lapham] and I slept with Newell Slauson in Co. B. Co H was scattered all over the reg't for food and lodging.

Oct. 29. Paymaster Hunt came and also Co's E & D from Chattanooga.

Oct. 30. Set up until 1 o'clock at night to make out a new pay roll. One of my eyes was somewhat inflamed.

Oct. 31. Was mustered out the U.S. service about noon. We did not receive our discharge papers. More rolls had to be made out but my eye was so bad I got excused.

Nov. 1. We received four months pay in the afternoon. I received $72.00.

Nov. 2. It rained all night. A building burned about daylight. We drew guns and accoutrements to take with us for self defense in Nashville.

Nov. 3. It was cold and stormy. Our band escorted us to the train about 11 A.M. There were two trains loaded with artillery ammunition and we had orders to get on top of the cars. My sore eye got me in the hospital car which was more comfortable. But little growling was heard as it meant going home. Co. H were put on the first train. At Marietta nearly all the boys got inside the cars on account of the cold.

Nov. 4. Morning found us in Cartersville. I did not sleep a wink all night it was so cold and the cars so crowded.

Nov. 5. I got a little sleep but not to exceed an hour. Found ourselves in Dalton at daylight and stayed there until noon then went by way of Cleveland. Had to cut the wood and dip the water for our engine. Had quite a row with some cavalry on the train. One struck Dan Brown in the face with his saber, making quite a wound. Reached Cleveland at sundown and remained until 9 P.M. I got a good supper at the hotel for 75 cts. A part of the train jumped the track twice during the day and cars and locomotives were frequently seen in the ditches wrecked.

Nov. 6. Reached Chattanooga at 2 A.M. The second train at 7 A.M. Took up quarters in an old warehouse near a lot of conscripts and substitutes for whom we had a hearty contempt. Drew rations and were very comfortable. Rained hard all night and was very muddy.

Nov. 7. Felt much better after a good nights sleep. My other eye began to get sore. Col Innes and Hunton went to Nashville.

Nov. 8. When Cap and I began to dress, our boots were missing. We set them on a beam under our head and some rascal climbed up in the night and captured them. We each borrowed a pair until we got to Nashville. We loaded ourselves on the cars without orders and the officers followed us. Left at 11 A.M. and rode all the way on top of the cars. Dr. DeCamp opened the polls for us to vote. I cast my first vote and for Abe Lincoln for president at Stevenson in mud nearly up to my knees. But 103 votes were cast.

Nov. 9. Arrived in Nashville about 9 A.M. and hungry, not daring to sleep for fear we would roll off the cars and be killed. Turned over our guns and might have gone on had the officers tried to secure our transportation. I slept on the floor in the Court House. They tried to get us to go to the Zollicoffer House or the "Louse House" as the boys called it. Paid our own board bills at the hotels. Had orders to be ready to go at 7 A.M. tomorrow.

Nov. 10. We were at the depot on time and a train of passenger cars were waiting but no officers or orders. Their excuse was the transportation papers were not made out. The boys were much excited and it would take but little to start a big row. We finally got in some box cars and left at 5 P.M. Stopped in Edgefield and then went on.

Nov. 11. Had breakfast at Elizabethtown and reached Louisville at 1 P.M. Marched to the ferry and loaded on the boat to cross the river into "Gods" Country, as the boys termed it. Col Hunton had the papers for two darkies to cross but as he was not there we were detained about an hour.[2]

Nov. 12. Woke up in Indianapolis. Had our breakfast and looked around the city considerably. Left at 1 P.M. on the Indianapolis and Belfontaine R.R. Had passenger cars. Some of the boys were drunk and got left. Reached Sydney about midnight.

Nov. 13. Changed cars for the Dayton & Mich R.R. Arrived in Toledo at 10 A.M. and again changed for Detroit. Arrived within a mile of the city when the engine jumped the track and we had to foot it about two miles to the Dutch Theatre, which was regimental Hdqrs, and then we went for something to eat. Had the citizens been aware of our coming a reception and dinner would have been waiting for us. Women would wave their handkerchiefs at us but we did not show the enthusiasm over such things we did three years before. A few of us went to the City Hotel where we had excellent accommodations.

Nov. 14. Charley and I had to make some changes in the payroll and they were then signed. Bought a suit of clothes for $75.00, exclusive of boots, hat, and pants and they were nothing extra at that price. Had a good bath and attended theatre at night.

Nov. 15. Expected pay and went to Hd Qrs for that purpose, but no officers were there. Finally some came and said we would not be paid until tomorrow. The boys got hot over that again as it was expensive for us to stop there.

2. The two men, former slaves, were servants to the officers.

Nov. 16. Reported we would not be paid today but finally received orders to meet opposite the P.O at 1 p.m. About two they began to pay by letter as the Cos were known in the reg't The paymasters money gave out when Co. H was paid and Cos I & K had to remain another day. Paid my bill at the hotel.

Nov. 17. Hired a dray to carry our trunks to the depot. Ten of us going toward Jackson took seats in the car. The rest, thinking the train would back in for another car, waited and got left. I got off at Sandstone and reached home once more about 1 p.m. and it was a happy reunion. Father was in Jackson and brought up my trunk.

Kimball returned to his father's farm and remained in the area until 1873. At some point after the war, he purchased a small farm just north of his father's and worked the land. He married twenty-four-year-old Laura Fellows on July 10, 1873. She was a schoolteacher and daughter of early Jackson County pioneers. Days after marrying, they moved to Mason County, Michigan, settling near the growing lumbering town of Ludington.

Ludington, soon incorporated as a city of some thirty-five hundred, occupied an enviable position as an important port city on Lake Michigan, aided greatly by the arrival of the railroad in 1874. The town's location at the mouth of the Pere Marquette River ensured that rapid growth soon followed, driven by the lumber industry and the city's mills and harbor. William H. Kimball quickly found work as a carpenter and then tallyman in the lumber mills. From there he moved up to lumber inspector and continued to work for major mills and timber companies in the Ludington area.

Daughter Eva was born in April 1874 and died two months later of whooping cough. Two sons followed—Horton Fellows in December 1878 and John Augustus in February 1887.

By the 1890s, Kimball was well known in the community, and he turned his efforts to politics. He was elected Mason County sheriff as a Republican in 1894 and reelected two years later. The Kimball family moved into Ludington proper, settling in a home near the county courthouse. William was eventually elected alderman in Ludington and then served several terms as city treasurer, remaining in office until 1916.

W. H. KIMBALL.

This image of Kimball after the war appeared in a turn-of-the-century community directory and promotional booklet. (Mason County Historical Society, Historic White Pine Village, Ludington, Michigan. Image reproduced and enhanced by Elizabeth Tiffany.)

Kimball was also active in local veterans' affairs, belonging for many years to Pap Williams Post, no. 15, Grand Army of the Republic (GAR), in which he held several leadership positions. The GAR, the preeminent organization for Civil War Union veterans, established itself as a major political and cultural force in late nineteenth- and early twentieth-century America. Kimball also transferred his Masonic membership from Jackson to Ludington and remained active in the local lodge until his death.

In 1898, the United States declared war on Spain, and war fever again infected the nation. Kimball's son Horton enlisted in Company A, Thirty-fifth Michigan Infantry and was eventually promoted to sergeant. His unit organized just as active fighting during the short war was ending. While negotiators were working on final peace terms, the regiment was moved first to Pennsylvania and then eventually to Augusta, Georgia, where it was mustered out at the end of March 1899.

Horton returned from the war to Ludington and worked as a dentist. He later moved to Idaho and practiced there for a few years before relocating to Detroit, where he was still living in the 1930s. Younger brother John, also a dentist, eventually made his move to Idaho, remaining there well into the 1940s.

William H. Kimball died on October 30, 1920, after a long illness. He was laid to rest in Lakeview Cemetery in Ludington after a large funeral with full military honors. His widow, Laura, died the following year and was buried alongside. Their two sons and their wives are also buried in Lakeview Cemetery in Ludington.

William Horton Kimball's headstone in Ludington's Lakeview Cemetery. The birth year is probably in error according to other sources, including his journal entry of December 1, 1863, which notes his twenty-first birthday on that date. (Elizabeth Tiffany)

Appendix

---◆---

KIMBALL'S COMRADES

---◆---

These individuals were among Kimball's closest comrades during his service or people whom he otherwise referenced frequently. Unless noted, all soldiers were members of Company H, First Michigan Engineers and Mechanics

---◆---

Daniel Bennett. Prewar neighbor and friend of Kimball's. Enlisted with Kimball, Bennett not quite eighteen years of age at the time. Served from 1861 to 1864. Lived in Michigan and Colorado after the war and died in 1929 in Royal Oak, Michigan.

Daniel B. and William H. Brown. Brothers and prewar neighbors of Kimball's. Enlisted with him in 1861, Daniel age twenty-six and William age thirty-three. Both were farmers before the war. Left the regiment with Kimball in the fall of 1864 after three years of service. Their younger brother Charles married Kimball's sister Amelia in 1864. Both Daniel and William lived in Jackson County after the war. Daniel survived until 1908 and is buried in Chapel Cemetery, Jackson County. William died in 1905 and is buried in nearby Dearing Cemetery, Jackson County.

Hiram Casler. Kimball usually misspells surname as Cassler. Prewar resident of Eaton County; returned there after the war to farm. Served with Kimball from 1861 to 1864. Later served briefly at war's end in the

Tenth Michigan Cavalry. Died in 1919 in Eaton Rapids and is buried in Maple Hill Cemetery, Charlotte, Eaton County.

Merrick Chamberlain. Kimball usually refers to him as Mic. Prewar laborer in Jackson County. Enlisted on Sept 30, 1861, age nineteen, and was discharged at the expiration of his term of service on October 31, 1864. Lived in Jackson County until his death in 1891, working at various times as a carpenter and druggist, and is buried in Spring Arbor Cemetery.

Harry J. Chapel. Prewar resident of Adrian, Lenawee County. Enlisted as first sergeant on September 23, 1861, age twenty-eight. He was commissioned second lieutenant in January 1862 and then first lieutenant January 1864. Discharged at the expiration of his term of service on October 31, 1864. Lived in Michigan, New York, and Ohio after the war. Died about 1908, probably in Toledo.

Osmer Eaton. First name also listed as Orasmus. Prominent merchant in Otsego, Allegan County, before the war. Had traveled to California during the gold rush. Commissioned second lieutenant in Company H, effective January 1, 1864, age about fifty-four. Resigned and left in October 1864 with Kimball and the original members of the company. Returned to Allegan County and died there in 1885. Buried in Mountain Home Cemetery.

Charles W. Fowler. Farm laborer and Kimball's neighbor before the war. Enlisted with Kimball in 1861 and also returned with the original men in the fall of 1864. Farmed in Jackson County until his death in 1905. He is buried in Spring Arbor Cemetery.

Peter Gordon Jr. Prewar resident of Flint, where he enlisted on August 30, 1861, age thirty-three. Served until February 1864 when he accepted a commission as second lieutenant in the Sixteenth U.S. Colored Infantry. Resigned soon after and returned to Genesee County, where he died in 1923. Buried in Avondale Cemetery in Flint.

Marcus Grant. The Grant family were neighbors, and the Kimball farm had originally been developed by Reuben Grant. In 1860 Marcus Grant was working as a farm laborer in nearby Concord. Served as corporal in the First Michigan (three months) from April to August 1861. Though only twenty-two years old, he was commissioned as captain of

Company H in September 1861. Promoted to major in August 1864 and remained with the regiment until mustering out in September 1865. Remained in Tennessee as a railroad official and businessman for almost three decades before moving to Colorado in an effort to recover his health. Died in Denver in 1896 and is buried in the Chattanooga National Cemetery.

Solon E. Grant. Kinsman, though not brother, of Marcus Grant. Was working for a carpenter in 1860. Served in the First Michigan (three months) before being commissioned as second lieutenant of Company H in September 1861, age twenty-five. Promoted to first lieutenant and served until his resignation for disability in July 1863. Returned to Jackson and worked as a clerk before moving west to Kansas, where he died in 1879. Buried in Mt. Hope Cemetery, Independence, Kansas.

Ayres Merrill Grosvenor. Michigan native and resident of Jackson County. Enlisted in September 1861, age nineteen, and served for three years. Seriously wounded at Perryville. Returned to Michigan and farmed in Jackson, Kent, and Montcalm counties. Died 1914 in Montcalm County and is buried in Forest Home Cemetery, near Greenville.

Enos Hopkins. Born in Connecticut. Prewar businessman in Jackson with extensive experience in Connecticut's iron manufacturing trade. Raised the Withington Guards, which became Company H, Michigan Engineers. Commissioned major on September 12, 1861, age forty. Resigned May 1863. Kimball speaks favorably of his leadership during the pay dispute. Hopkins led the battalion of Michigan Engineers engaged at Perryville, which Kimball describes. He remained in Tennessee for a decade, serving for a time as postmaster of Nashville. Moved back east and remained active in business, dying in New York in 1896. Buried in his hometown of Naugatuck, Connecticut.

Henry House. Farm laborer from near Brooklyn, Jackson County. Enlisted in Company H September 23, 1861, age twenty-one. Died of disease at Murfreesboro, Tennessee, on April 23, 1863. Buried in Stones River National Cemetery. Kimball writes movingly of his death.

Charles Hoyer. German immigrant, a mason in Jackson before the war. Enlisted in September 1861 and served three years. Returned to

Jackson County and continued his trade. He died there in 1918 and is buried in Mt. Evergreen Cemetery in Jackson.

Kinsman A. Hunton. Master mechanic and superintendent of the Michigan Central Railroad's repair shops in Marshall. Original lieutenant colonel of the regiment and remained in that role until leaving with Innes in the fall of 1864. Moved to Chicago after the war, was a druggist, and died there in 1885.

William P. Innes. New York native and successful civil engineer in Grand Rapids, working primarily on railroads. Commanded the regiment from the fall of 1861 until resigning and leaving with Kimball and the other original members in the fall of 1864. Returned to Tennessee during Reconstruction and then again moved back to Grand Rapids, achieving continued success and prominence in business and community affairs. Died in 1893 and buried in Fulton Street Cemetery, Grand Rapids.

Edd Lapham. Variously appears in sources as Edmund or Edward. Enlisted in March 1863, age thirty-six. Justice of the peace in Brooklyn, Jackson County. Discharged in October 1865. Returned to Michigan. Died after 1889.

Joseph P. Lapham. Kimball refers to him as "Cap" for reasons that are unclear. Kinsman of Edd Lapham, but probably not his brother. Lived near Brooklyn in 1860, working as a farm laborer. Enlisted in September 1861 and served for three years. Returned to Jackson County and farmed near Norvell. Died before 1892.

Newell Slawson. Kimball's second cousin, their mothers being first cousins. Kimball spells surname Slauson; military records and tombstone have Slawson. Born in New York circa 1842 and living in Michigan's Montcalm County before the war. Like Kimball, served from 1861 to 1864 then returned to Michigan. Lived in Kent County after the war, but died in Texas in 1882. His body was returned to Kent County and he is buried in Elmwood Cemetery in Cedar Springs.

Albert Vanderwarker. Surname is also spelled Vandewarker in various sources, and Kimball often calls him "Vandy." Prewar resident of Washtenaw County. Original member of Company H, he enlisted at twenty and rose through the ranks. Eventually commissioned as first lieutenant in January 1864. He left with Kimball and the original men in the fall of 1864. Lived postwar in Jackson and Washtenaw counties and died in 1923. Buried in Reynolds Corner Cemetery, Washtenaw County.

George Waldo. Arrived in Michigan shortly before the war. Enlisted in September 1861, age thirty-one, and served through October 1864. Returned to Michigan and settled in Mecosta County, farming until his 1909 death in Big Rapids. He is buried in Ladner Cemetery.

Abner J. Walker. Kimball refers to him as "Doc." Ingham County farmer before the war. Enlisted in November 1861, age twenty-one, and served through October 1864. Returned to Michigan and took up the cobbler's trade in Washtenaw and Ingham counties. Died 1888 in Mason.

John B. Yates. Engineering graduate from Union College in New York. Civil engineer living in Albion. Michigan, in 1860. Original captain of Company A, age twenty-eight. Later promoted to major and then replaced Innes as colonel. Involved in railroad, canals, and other engineering projects postwar in New York and across United States and Canada. Died in Ontario in 1899 while under contract with the U.S. government for improvements along the St. Clair River. Buried in Vale Cemetery, in his native Schenectady, New York.

Bibliographic Essay

There are several sources for Kimball's life before and after the Civil War. These include "Biographical Sketch," William H. Kimball Papers, Burton Historical Collection, Detroit Public Library; Spring Arbor Historical Commission, *Spring Arbor Township, 1830–1980* (Spring Arbor, Mich.: Spring Arbor Historical Commission, 1980), 100–101; Works Progress Administration, comp., *Jackson County Family History* (n.p., 1936), 132–34; obituary in the *Ludington Morning News,* October 31, 1920, 1; and Perry F. Powers, *A History of Northern Michigan and Its Peoples, 1857–1945* (Chicago: Lewis, 1912), 711–12. Kimball's involvement in the Grand Army of the Republic is drawn from records of the Pap Williams Post, no. 15, GAR Records, in the Archives of Michigan, Lansing. Additional information is found in files of the Historic White Pine Village in Ludington, operated by the Mason County Historical Society.

The most complete account of Kimball's regiment is the author's *My Brave Mechanics: The First Michigan Engineers and Their Civil War* (Detroit: Wayne State University Press, 2007). Additional information, including several photos used in this publication, is in Charles R. Sligh, *History of the Services of the First Regiment Michigan Engineers and Mechanics, during the Civil War, 1861–1865* (Grand Rapids, Mich.: White, 1921).

There are many accounts of the Civil War in the Kentucky-Tennessee theater where Kimball served, but the following were particularly helpful: Larry J. Daniel, *Days of Glory: The Army of the Cumberland, 1861–1865* (Baton Rouge: Louisiana University Press, 2004); James

Lee McDonough, *War in Kentucky: From Shiloh to Perryville* (Knoxville: University of Tennessee Press, 1994); Kenneth W. Noe, *Perryville: This Grand Havoc of Battle* (Lexington: University Press of Kentucky, 2001); and Frank Welcher, *The Union Army, 1861–1865: Organization and Operations,* vol. 2 (Bloomington: Indiana University Press, 1993).

The theme of civilian response to military occupation is thoroughly discussed in several excellent studies, most notably Mark Grimsley, *The Hard Hand of War: Union Military Policy toward Southern Civilians, 1861– 1865* (New York: Cambridge University Press, 1995); and two books by Stephen V. Ash, *When the Yankees Came: Conflict and Chaos in the Occupied South, 1861–1865* (Chapel Hill: University of North Carolina Press, 1995) and *Middle Tennessee Society Transformed, 1860–1870: War and Peace in the Upper South* (Knoxville: University of Tennessee Press, 1988). Two recent additions to this field of study from Louisiana State University Press are Bradley R. Clampitt, *The Confederate Heartland: Military and Civilian Morale in the Western Confederacy* (2011) and LeeAnn Whites and Alecia P. Long, *Occupied Women: Gender, Military Occupation, and the American Civil War* (2009). The shift to a harder-war policy has been most effectively summarized by James M. McPherson in *Tried by War: Abraham Lincoln as Commander in Chief* (New York: Penguin, 2008), especially 103–7.

Several sources provided the basis for most of the information on individuals with whom Kimball served, including those in the appendix. These sources include U.S. Census schedules for 1850 to 1930; *Record of Service of Michigan Volunteers in the Civil War,* vol. 43 (Kalamazoo, Mich.: Ihling Bros. and Everard, 1904); and the collections of the National Archives, Washington, D.C., especially pension files in Record Group 15 and regimental papers in Record Group 94. Burial information is from the author's personal surveys, various cemetery transcriptions, and the online graves database of the Sons of Union Veterans of the Civil War.

Index of Names and Places